"*Miracles* drew n⁣ ⁣'d
to put down as a⁣ ⁣h
everyone at a pc⁣ ⁣.g,
to those who are sure of their faith, and everyone between. While easy to read, it takes the reader on a captivating and challenging journey through the ambiguity of life as we experience it, and connects to our own beliefs about God and life. Seldom do I find a book I could see sharing with anyone. This one I will."

–Ray Vander Kooij
Senior Pastor, Bethel Christian Reformed Church
Acton, Ontario

"There is nothing like a true story to bring the truth of Scripture to life. John has done a masterful job at weaving together what God has said in the past, and what God is doing in the present. This book is a God-centered, Jesus-focused, Spirit-empowered account that will stimulate your faith, challenge your complacency; nourish your soul and stir your heart. *Miracles* provides a helpful framework in answering key questions we all have on the journey. Read it and allow God to take you deeper on your journey of faith."

–Dr. Justin Dennison
Lead Pastor, Johnston Heights Church
Surrey, British Columbia

"In our post-rational age when the non-Western world is moving in on the West, we are facing the need for a new apologetic–a new defence of the Christian faith. The modern days of scientific and intellectual evidences which caused us to ask the question "Does God exist?" have been replaced by the post-modern days in which the apologetic question now heard is, "Does God do anything?" This, effectively, is the challenge put to Christianity by both non-Christians and other religions.

Miracles delivers powerful answers by way of stories and accounts of what God is doing. John's further reflections on the subject are honest and heartfelt; they bring the reader to an understanding of his own concerns as to God's disposition towards us. The reader is guided toward a normative relationship and walk with the Father. In this honest and courageous work, John provides pastoral guidance from a wealth of experience as a student of the Word, as a family person, and as one who has had ample opportunity to serve as a chronicler of the stories of our brothers and sisters in Eastern Europe."

–Ian Campbell
Lead Pastor, Grandview Baptist Church
Kitchener, Ontario

"Over the course of our lives we have all asked the questions found in this book... John Murray looks squarely at the subjects raised and builds answers on the strength of sound biblical knowledge. This book will be a source of great encouragement and a real faith-builder to all who read it. I highly recommend it to the believer, as well as those seeking to understand the Christian faith."

–Rev. Dr. Douglas Coombs
Chairman of the Board, Eurovangelism Canada

MIRACLES:
COINCIDENCE OR DIVINE INTERVENTION?

JOHN MURRAY

TOUCH
PUBLISHING

Copyright © 2014 by C. John Murray

All rights reserved. No portion of this book may be reproduced, stored in a retrieval system, or transmitted in any form or by any means—electronic, mechanical, photocopy, recording, or any other—without prior written consent from the publisher.

Scripture taken from the Holy Bible, New International Version®, NIV®, Copyright© 1973, 1978, 1984 by the International Bible Society, Used by permission of Zondervan Publishing House, The "NIV" and "New International Version" trademarks are registered in the United States Patent and Trademark Office by International Bible Society.

Published by Touch Publishing
P.O. Box 180303
Arlington, Texas 76096
www.TouchPublishingServices.com

ISBN 978-0-9937951-7-6

Printed in the United States of America on acid-free paper

Library of Congress Control Number: 2014950444

To Rita,
my wonderful wife and friend,
who tirelessly and lovingly
has given me encouragement and support
these past fifty years.

CONTENTS

PREFACE

Is there such a thing as coincidence or is life orchestrated by an invisible hand? At times when the unexpected happens, especially to our benefit, is it a chance event or was it meant to happen on our behalf?

The Oxford Dictionary defines coincidence as a "remarkable concurrence of events apparently by chance." The last part is particularly significant: "apparently by chance." This leaves the door open for it *not* being by chance.

When we experience what we consider to be a coincidence in life we mostly accept it as such, and allow it to pass by without giving it much attention. However, when the coincidence has a spiritual element to it, we then begin to give it a second thought and wonder whether it was a coincidence or something more like divine intervention.

Have you ever experienced an unexpected solution to a problem? I have. I've experienced unforeseen funds turn up from a stranger to meet a financial crisis. Have you have people cross your path and you sense that it was no accident? How about when someone seemingly arrives from nowhere and is in the right place at the right time to avert serious injury to a family member? How do you view these occurrences? If there is a spiritual aspect to the event, it naturally causes us to look and think more deeply about its significance.

What are our choices in this matter? Either an extraordinary event or happening turns out to be pure coincidence or it is of divine origin. If the second, then it has to be classified as a miracle. Again the dictionary takes a non-committal position by saying that a miracle is an event which is "supposedly supernatural"–which is quite nebulous. If an occurrence has no rational or natural explanation, then it has to be supernatural. If supernatural, then it is miraculous because any intervention of God in the life of an individual is a miracle.

God created the world and in so doing set in process the laws of nature. We are all subject to those laws and the consequences of the natural process of life, whether we are Christians or not. However, because God brought the natural laws into existence, He has the right to override those laws and can choose to make them non-effective–hence the realm of miracles.

Simply put, miracles occur when God chooses for them to occur; although we may think them to be coincidences. But if that were always the case then some of us Christians have been subjected to a myriad of coincidences in our lives, wouldn't we? Because God is sovereign, all-knowing, and all-powerful, He can intervene in the lives of humans at will.

When the divine intersects with humanity, it will result in an event which is normally inexplicable by man. God is not God *because* He performs miracles. He performs miracles because He is God. Miracles do not make Him who He is, but it is because of who He is that he performs miracles.

This book is about miracles because it is a book about God's intervention in the lives of ordinary people. Some of the stories are personal, others are about people I know, while still others have come from first-hand sources. The book was written as a faith-builder and as a means of encouragement in the Christian walk. If you are looking to be encouraged and have your faith strengthened by seeing God at work, then this book is for you.

If, on the other hand, you have doubts about the occurrence of miracles, that's fine. You read the book and determine for yourself whether there are such things as miracles or should these extraordinary events be written off as coincidence? You decide.

A NOTE ON GROUP STUDY

The subjects covered in this book are rich for group discussion. At the end of each chapter you will find questions for that purpose. Prayerfully consider the questions, and be encouraged by stories of God's intervention in the lives of other group members.

As well as promoting a good discussion, hopefully, these questions will help in the personal application of the Scriptural principles learned. Ask God to apply them to your life, so that you might grow in understanding and in your Christian faith.

CHAPTER ONE:
DOES GOD CARE?

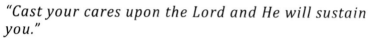

"Cast your cares upon the Lord and He will sustain you."

Psalm 55:22

I have a friend who came from an extremely dysfunctional family. Both parents tragically committed suicide and he, together with his sister, was brought up by an aunt and uncle. They did their best. They showed him love and did what they thought was right–even sending him to church. However, underneath the surface of my friend's façade was repressed anger of huge proportions. He was like a volcano ready to explode. Eventually, it could be contained no longer and it all spilled over, setting him on an emotional and physical downward spiral. The events within that spiral took him into the world of sex, drugs, and self-abuse. More than once, he considered following in the path of his parents.

Yet, he tells me that when he reached the bottom, although blatantly angry with God, he knew that God was there and that somehow He cared. He certainly did not think or feel that God *showed* He cared. In fact, it was just the opposite–he felt totally abandoned by God. Yet, deep down, there was an inner knowledge of God's concern that kept him from self-destruction. His road eventually led back to a life of somewhat normality. However, contentment eluded him until God began to bring Christian people across his path; people who gave tangible evidence that they cared about him. At first, he was skeptical and unconvinced by their efforts, but the love and care continued. He decided to bring up his most complex questions about God and the Christian faith, all of which were met with the same undeterred love and consideration.

It's been eleven years since he was at "the bottom." Today, he and his family are within the family of God. His understanding of the Christian faith and theology would leave many of us far behind. In fact, he is now in Seminary as a mature student, training for the ministry. His life is a testimony to God's love, redemption, and care. Yet look at the path he had to tread; a path most of us would not want to know or experience. Through it all, he maintains that God cared for him, even when he did not care for himself.

When we ask the question, "Does God care?" we are also questioning His love. It is impossible for us to love someone and not care for them. The two go together. To love someone is to care about what happens to them. The apostle John tells us in his epistle that "God is love" (1 John 4:8), which means love is His character and love emanates from His very Being. It is difficult to question the love of a God who gave His only Son to die for people who were rebellious against Him. Because God extended such unconditional love and grace to the world, it makes raising the question of His care for us virtually inconsequential, or worse, an insult. God cares for us even when we are unaware of it, when we don't feel it, and even when we cannot comprehend it.

Life revolves around us. It is natural that we ask, "Does God care about me?" Whatever happens to us and around us is what affects us; and it is usually only when we are adversely affected by life's circumstances that the question of God's care arises. Otherwise we think little about it.

When we are looking for God's care we usually add another question. It is the "Why me?" question. When we go through physical and emotional trials, this age-old question is never far from the surface. This leads to others: "Why didn't God protect me from this situation?" We even think such things as, "I am trying to do all I should as a Christian, why do things still go wrong?" Subconsciously, we think that we must perform to earn the blessing of God and that by "doing things" we receive blessings which guarantee to keep us from sickness, danger, and adverse situations. Sadly, somehow we have acquired this erroneous theology along the way. We are not on a spiritual performance treadmill to please God or to earn His favor. He does not grant or withhold His blessings because of our spiritual activity or lack of it. God grants us blessings and answers to prayer because of His love and grace.

God loves us unconditionally. We cannot make Him love us more, and we cannot make Him love us less. We are recipients of His love and grace without having to make any contribution. In Romans chapter five, Paul tells us that Christ died for us while we were sinners (Romans 5:8). If God gave His Son to die in our place while we were in our sin, why would God think less of us, or stop loving us, if we disappoint Him now?

When my wife was diagnosed with cancer, my first thought was, "Why you?" Yet when I mentioned it to her, her reply was, "Why *not* me?" I had never thought of it that way. She was living out the concept that this diagnosis was no surprise to God; therefore He must have a greater purpose in mind. As it happened, she was right. She experienced a miraculous healing which took place overnight, much to the amazement of the surgeon. Her story of healing is elsewhere in this book.

Few of us can escape crises. Life is hard when we suffer as a result of an illness or an accident. Life is difficult when we have to endure economic hardship because of losing a job or we find it challenging to exist on a limited income. Being unfairly or unjustly treated is also tough to accept. However, as someone once said, "If everyone put their problems and circumstances in a circle on the floor, and we could choose what we wanted, when we saw what others were going through, we'd be down there retrieving what we had to begin with."

None of us like to be criticized, especially if we consider the criticism to be unwarranted. Our natural inclination is to defend ourselves. We attempt to rationalize what we said or how we behaved. If that doesn't do the job, we might even start hitting back at the one who had thrown the criticism our way. However, although criticism is hurtful and painful to us, it is miniscule in comparison to persecution! I sometimes wonder how I would handle outright persecution. If ever there was a situation where the question of "Why me?" or "Why us?" would appear to be justified, it would be by the Church under persecution.

Historically, persecution is not foreign to the Church. Just look at *Foxe's Book of Martyrs* to see how many Christians in history were burned at the stake for their faith. We also see in Scripture a disturbing list of those who were mutilated and suffered immensely because of their faithfulness to God. In Hebrews we read, "...others were tortured and refused to be released, so that they might gain a better resurrection. Some faced jeers and flogging, while still others were chained and put in prisons. They were stoned, they were sawed in two; they were put to death by the sword..." (Hebrews 11:35-37). It makes for horrific reading, and it verifies that throughout the ages, God's people have suffered for their faith; and we wonder, if God cares, why does He allow such atrocities?

For seventy years in Russia and forty years in Eastern Europe, the Church went through the fires of persecution. Regrettably, as time passes we hear less about this particular period in the Church, as new persecution stories replace them, but nevertheless it was very real for those who experienced it. The atheistic political stronghold of communism came into power in the Soviet Union in 1917. This ultimately became the authoritative rule in all the East bloc countries, which came under the domination of the Soviet Union after World War II. Consequently, until the last of these governments collapsed (which was Albania in 1991), the Church was subject to untold oppression and open persecution. This was not just a case of inconvenience through officious obstacles, but deliberate opposition to the existence of the Church, and to individual Christians who were restricted from openly practicing their faith.

However, the Church in Eastern Europe has not been alone in its subjection to persecution. The Church in many places around the world has suffered, and is still suffering wickedness and humiliation for simply exercising the Christian faith–a right we take for granted in the West. It has been stated that there were more martyrs for the faith during the 20th century than any other century in history. This highlights how enormously widespread persecution is today against the Church worldwide.

I know that Jesus forewarned of this when He said, "If they persecuted me, they will persecute you also..." (John 15:20); but it is still difficult for us in our humanness to come to terms with this suffering within the Church. Many questions come to mind: Where was God when this happened? Why did He let it happen? Why did He not intervene? Did He not care for His children? Was it not His Church which suffered? Was it not His children that were being imprisoned, tortured, and murdered?

These are not easy questions to answer. What we do know is that God does not always intervene as we think He should, nor when we think He should, or even act as we think He should. Maybe Isaiah sheds some light on this when he quotes God who says, "For my thoughts are not your thoughts, neither are my ways your ways" (Isaiah 55:8).

We live in the physical and material world. We see what we think are the results of God not intervening. We experience the disappointment, the heartache, the emotional turmoil of tragic events in our lives. In those times, we wish above everything else that we might see God decisively putting His hand upon our situation and making the changes that we so desire. I am sure it was the same for those Christians in Eastern Europe as they suffered mercilessly at the hands of the communist authorities. They probably could not understand it anymore than we can today. On the surface it would appear that God had virtually abandoned the Church and His children, while they endured, survived, or succumbed to the onslaught of such satanic forces. But was that really true?

Even the Children Suffered

At the height of the Romanian Government's obsession with eradicating the Christian faith, they even persecuted children. One newsletter that related activities of the State against the Church told the story of a small girl named Delia. She was no more than ten years old and came from a Christian home. Each day she would walk to school with fists clenched, and praying as she went: "Lord Jesus, help me!" One morning, she was checked into school as usual by two teachers at the door before she moved on into her classroom. The 30 plus children stood to attention waiting for the teacher to come into the room.

The teacher did not come alone. With her was the headmaster, whom the children dreaded, followed by another teacher, and behind them came a policeman with high boots and a gun. The children were afraid, not knowing what was about to happen. They were told to sit down and put their hands behind their backs. Delia again clenched her fists, still praying her prayer, "Lord Jesus, help me!"

The next moment, she heard her name being called: "Comrade Ionescu! Stand up and come here!"

Delia got up and went forward, her face pale.

"Where were you on Friday? Answer!" came the headmaster's booming voice. Looking down, Delia did not answer... she couldn't even move her lips. She was shaking all over. She knew that a few evenings previously she had been in the home of a Sunday school teacher who had shown them slides about Jesus, and, when they had finished, the police arrived, confiscated the slides and the projector, and had taken their names. Since then, she had been very afraid. Delia heard the headmaster going on and on in front of the class, who were silent and obviously very scared.

Then, warning them about going with Christians anywhere, the policeman said, "These Christians like Ionescu do not obey the laws of the State and the laws of the Party. They are lazy and even try to influence others. You should never go with them!"

"Whom did you take with you the other evening, Comrade Ionescu? Answer!" the headmaster's stern voice rang out again. But Delia was as white as a sheet and did not answer. The headmaster, hearing no reply, grabbed Delia by the hair and shook her furiously a few times, then pushed her away. All the children held their breath as they saw Delia fall to the floor and faint. The "guests" then left the classroom and the teacher brought a glass of water and sprinkled it on Delia's face to revive her. She was put on a bench and left there, and after some time she came round. The children in the class watched her, scared and silent.

But Delia now had a serene and peaceful look on her face and, turning to her classmates and teacher, smiled and said, "I dreamt that the Lord Jesus came into the classroom and gave me a garland of flowers. He was so nice... and smiled at me."

The children and the teacher listened attentively, watching her in silence. That day Delia was the only child in the classroom who smiled.

To smile after such humiliating circumstances forces us to think that it was impossible for her to do so in her own strength. Did God care for Delia? I believe He did. However, He did not keep her from the nasty experience of being humiliated before her classmates. God did not deliver her from the mistreatment or the fear of reprisal, as we might have thought He should, but He comforted her with a reassuring dream which gave her a supernatural peace. Her confidence in God would have been restored, if not increased. God does not always work the way we think He should, but He does always care for us.

Open persecution was not the only way that Romanian Christians suffered. Because food was scarce they, along with other families, lived daily with extreme deprivation. They lived at subsistence level. The dictator Ceauşescu was more interested in controlling his people than feeding them. One way that Christians in the West showed care and love for these families was by sending food parcels to them. You can imagine the appreciation. Most people would write back to express their thanks and gratitude. One such grateful recipient wrote the following letter:

"Together with my husband and five children, I thank you with all of my heart for the love which you have for us, and we thank God that He cares for us as a father for his children. When troubles overwhelm, God shows His great love.

"I, the mother of the children, became very ill at the birth of the last child, and I had to give up my job because of the illness. I have not been working for four years, but we thank God that we have never gone hungry. He has not left the children without their mother. With God everything is possible–only let us have great faith! Once again, we thank you for everything you sent us... Your brothers and sisters will not forget you."

Under trying conditions and extreme hardship God cares for His children, whether it is directly or through other believers. Although problems may continue and the circumstances remain hard, God provides, miraculously or otherwise. This sounds fine for the believer, but does God care for the non-believer?

God's Care for Non-believers

A story passed on to me from a missionary friend takes us to the jungles of Suriname. There, the native Indians live simply, surviving on plants and animals from the jungle. They live in small groups or bands and roam the jungle. Most have now been discovered by the outside world. However, a few years ago, some missionaries and native Indian Christians were attempting to make contact with one of the last groups to be discovered. To their amazement, when they tracked them down they found that the group had dwindled to one woman and her two children. When spotted, the three ran off into the jungle, afraid of the "foreigners." In their rush to get away from being captured, the young girl dropped their "fire," which was a piece of smouldering wood they needed for cooking, warmth, and safety from marauding jaguars. The search group retreated to their camp. However, during the night the girl crept into the camp to steal a piece of wood from their fire. She was caught by the Indian Christians who kept her until morning.

In the morning, the mother came out of the jungle to look for her daughter. She was delighted to see that no harm had come to her. The native Indians immediately engaged her in conversation. Her name was Irita and it seemed that she had been starved of adult conversation for a very long time and was pleased to chat. One of her stories was astounding.

Because she had lost her husband, she alone was responsible for finding food and providing protection for her children. She told how she had climbed high up into a tree to collect honey. She slipped and fell and said that she should have died, but first one branch broke her fall, then another, and another until she landed on the ground, bruised but with no major injury. Shortly after, they were stalked by a large jaguar. Naturally, it is impossible to outrun such animals, so Irita huddled together with her children, resigned to the fact that death was about to come upon them. She waited for the jaguar to pounce. Then a strange thing occurred.

Irita said that when nothing happened, she opened her eyes and there stood a man between her and the jaguar. The jaguar looked at the man and ran away. The man simply said to her, "People will be coming to tell you about me!"

When she related this to the missionaries and the native Indian Christians, the Indians became very excited, started dancing around and shouting, "That was God! That was God!"

Irita and her children became part of this group of Indians. After a number of months of experiencing the reality of the Christian faith in her newfound friends, she and her children made commitments to Christ and found that reality for themselves. Irita and her son died not many months later.

Did God care for Irita and her children even when they were not believers? Did God protect her life and the lives of her children from the jaguar? I believe God cares more than we can imagine. Why does the Scripture say He does not wish any man to perish but that all would come to understand the truth?

In Genesis 6, we read that God was grieved and His heart was filled with pain because man had become so evil. Why would He feel that way if He did not care? Jesus wept over the city of Jerusalem because of the people's spiritual ignorance and lack of response to the truth. His constant love and care for all men was seen throughout His ministry. He saw the crowds and had compassion on them. He healed those brought to Him without first asking if they believed. Jesus' love for all was obvious.

Peter says, "Cast all your anxiety on him because he cares for you" (1 Peter 5:7). We do God an injustice to even think or question His care for us. In the epistle of John we find these words, "God is love. This is how God showed his love among us; he sent his one and only son into the world that we might live through him. This is love; not that we loved God, but that he loved us and sent his son as an atoning sacrifice for our sins" (1 John 4:8-10). Do we need any more evidence of God's love and care for us?

Maybe you are in a situation that is painful or perhaps even devastating. Perhaps you have been badly hurt and you are feeling terribly alone or even abandoned. Let me assure you that you are not alone. God has promised, "I will never leave you, nor forsake you" (Hebrews 13:5). There are times when we have to remind ourselves again and again of that promise. Naturally, under adverse circumstances our feelings tell us differently, but our faith is built on facts and our feelings must take second place. The facts of God's love and faithfulness are permanent. Our feelings are temporary. God is the God who cares for His children. He cares for us more than we will ever know. We are not called to understand, but we are called to trust. God knows us. He understands us. He knows all about our circumstances and has made numerous promises to care for us. God has always been faithful to His Word and we have no reason to believe that will ever change.

GUIDE FOR GROUP STUDY

Chapter 1: Does God Care?

Bible reading: Psalm 139:13-18

*13 For you created my inmost being; you knit me
together in my mother's womb.
14 I praise you because I am fearfully and wonderfully
made; your works are wonderful, I know that full well.
15 My frame was not hidden from you when I was
made in the secret place, when I was woven together in
the depths of the earth.
16 Your eyes saw my unformed body;all the days
ordained for me were written in your book before one
of them came to be.
17 How precious to me are your thoughts, God! How
vast is the sum of them!
18 Were I to count them, they would outnumber the
grains of sand—when I awake, I am still with you.*

Questions for discussion:

1) Has life ever caused you to question God's care? What
was the outcome?

2) How do you think God shows His care? How have you
experienced such care? What, in your life, could help you
conclude that God does care for you?

3) How can you, in a practical manner, "cast your care" upon Him?

4) How do your feelings sometimes get in the way of your faith?

5) What can you do to constantly remind yourself that God loves you and cares for you unconditionally?

6) How can you show God's care to other people?

7) What can you do to encourage those who need to know that God cares for them?

CHAPTER TWO:
Does God Answer Prayer?

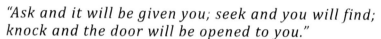

*"Ask and it will be given you; seek and you will find;
knock and the door will be opened to you."*
Matthew 7:7

In 1974, Romania was in the vice-grip of its dictator,
Nicolae Ceaușescu. The people lived in fear. Secret police
were everywhere; just waiting to pounce on anyone out of
line. Informants were even among your friends. It was
suggested at the time that one in three people were
informants, willing or otherwise. (Most would do anything
for an extra packet of cigarettes.) The Church was under
heavy scrutiny. It was severely restricted in its activity and
received open opposition—including the arrest and
interrogation of its pastors.

It was under these circumstances that a few women
from Emmanuel Baptist Church in Oradea, in northwest
Romania, felt the urge to pray for their country together on a
regular basis. They went to their pastor and requested the
use of a room at the church for prayer. They decided that

very early in the morning was best. The time was set for 5:30 a.m.

This handful of women began their prayer vigil and consistently met to pray for their country and the Church. It was not long before others heard about the prayer meeting and wanted to join in. Soon the room was not big enough to hold all of the people, so a larger room was allocated. This was followed by the need to use an even larger room, and then another, and another, until only the sanctuary was left in which to meet. What began as five women meeting together for prayer, finished with over 500 people meeting each morning to pray specifically for change to come about in their country of Romania. Most of the men attending would do so before going off to work. The pastor told me that Saturday was somewhat of a rest day, so the prayer meeting commenced at 8.00 a.m. instead of 5:30 a.m. Because most people did not go to work on that day, the number of people attending on Saturday would swell to 900.

The amazing aspect about this story is not that the prayer meeting occurred early each morning, or the increasing number of people who flocked to the church to pray before they went to work, but that this prayer meeting went on every day for fifteen years before they began to see answers to their prayers. While under heavy persecution, they had prayed that the time would come when the Church would be able to worship freely. They prayed for the freedom to share the Gospel with those outside the Church, and that it could be done openly on the streets. They prayed that evangelistic meetings would be held in cultural halls, and that Bibles would be plentiful and allowed to be distributed. All of this would have been absolutely impossible at that time, and virtually impossible even to imagine.

It was not until 1989 that the communist governments of Eastern Europe began to crumble and lose power. One by one: East Germany, Czechoslovakia (as it was then), Hungary —they fell like a house of cards, releasing their people from 40 years of communist oppression. On November 22, 1989, Ceauşescu, Romania's dictator, made a public speech to thousands of people. He boldly stated that, "What has taken place in other East European countries will never happen here!" On Christmas Day, just 33 days later, he and his wife were dead, executed by their own soldiers. Freedom came to the Church.

The very things that the people had prayed for in those early morning meetings came about. The Gospel was allowed to be openly preached on the streets—even to the holding of evangelistic crusades in soccer stadiums! Bibles were freely distributed and Christian literature was available for all. We in the West looked at the situation and thought it had been a successful revolution, but one pastor said, "What you people in the West call a revolution, we call divine intervention!"

I have often wondered how many of us in the West would have continued to pray for fifteen years with requests that appeared so incredibly impossible? It had to be a God-given vision for them to even bring to mind the possibility of seeing such a vast change in their country. God answered prayer and rewarded their faithfulness. Although having received the answers to prayer, they continued their regular prayer meetings for many years. When visitors from the West were invited to the early morning prayer meeting, they always went expecting to see a handful of deacons or other keen Christians, but were shocked to see the crowds going in for prayer at such an hour. Does God answer prayer? He certainly did for the Romanian Church.

Prayer in Prison

A number of years ago, my wife and I had a Romanian man stay with us in our home. This man's story had astounded the Church in the West. His story was one of undeniable injustice at the hands of the communist authorities. His name was Constantin, an ordinary man with a job and a family who was keen to help his pastor—especially in the distribution of Bibles. Early one evening, he borrowed his pastor's car to deliver some Bibles. Unfortunately, he was stopped by the police, which always resulted in a search of the car. They discovered the Bibles on the back seat.

Immediately he was told to get out of the car and was arrested for what he thought was "being in possession of Bibles." But that was not the charge. As he opened the door, it inadvertently swung open and hit one of the policemen, resulting in a scratch on the back of his hand. For that, Constantin was charged with the attempted murder of a police officer. He was sentenced to seven and a half years in prison.

His prison experience was horrific. His treatment was brutal. The dormitory held fifty men. They shared one toilet and two small wash basins. There was a constant line to use the facilities. They slept on iron beds, were given blankets full of bed bugs, and the lights were never turned off. The food was vile, but the prisoners were so hungry they would eat anything, including the worms or maggots in the rotting food. Breakfast came at 5:15 a.m. and consisted of one slice of bread and tea. Then, for lunch, they were given a small serving of corn mush (boiled maize), and a small helping of soup. This was served at 2:30 p.m. The evening meal arrived at 9:00 p.m. and usually consisted of a few spoonfuls of boiled wheat or vegetables.

Constantin recalls, "Before I went to prison, I'd had a history of stomach ulcers and colitis. I had been on a special diet for the last two or three years, but still suffered frequent pain caused by the condition. In prison, the Lord drew very close to me and miraculously healed me of this illness. I never had any pain or problems with the prison food. I count this as a real answer to the many prayers on my behalf."

The cells were so secure that guards had to unlock three doors to get in. Even so, they counted the prisoners twice a day; once at 7:00 a.m. and again at 7:00 p.m. At those times, the prisoners were forced to stand facing the wall. Their faces were only a few inches away from it. They would have to stand in that position for as long as it took the guards to reach their cell and count them. Often, this was two hours or more.

Again, in his own words, Constantin said, "At first 'facing the wall' was a time to be endured, but as the days went by it turned into a time of prayer and meditation, and talks with the Lord. I felt free from any human plans, desires, or ambitions—free from the world! It didn't matter to me anymore whether I lived or died. There was one desire in my heart, which was to please my Lord and to be with Him."

He indicated that the time against the wall became very special and he eventually looked forward to it as he spent time in the presence of God.

To say that prison life was harsh is a gross understatement. The threat of physical punishment, including torture, was never far away. The dormitories were rife with informers, people who would report on other prisoners to earn an early release. That made it virtually impossible to even have much open communication with others. One word spoken against the Romanian authorities or in question of your sentence meant certain punishment; the worst of which was solitary confinement. In solitary, prisoners were made to stand, without a break, from 5:00 a.m. until 10:00 p.m. on the cold cement floor in complete darkness. The floor was the toilet, and food was served every other day.

Constantin said that a boy in his dormitory, who was due to be released within a few days, became so weak that he could not get out of bed. The guards beat him until he was unconscious and then threw him onto the floor of a 'solitary' cell. The next morning he was found dead. Such was the cruelty in the prisons of Romania. Constantin himself was beaten with the leg of a table and underwent other physical tortures of which he could not share with anyone, not even his wife.

The Church in the West heard about the plight of Constantin and the injustice of his situation. Prayer vigils were organized and a writing campaign was instigated from both the United Kingdom and the United States. It was estimated that more than 5,000 letters were sent to the Romanian embassies of these two countries. This action surprised the Romanian authorities. His sentence was reviewed and ultimately he was released. He had served one year in prison. This proved how false the charges had been. However, there was a condition. He and his family had to leave the country. They were deported. The Romanian Government obviously considered their continued presence in the country an embarrassment. This is how he came to be visiting us in Canada. Constatin and his family ultimately settled in the United States.

God answered the prayers of His people and allowed Constantin to be released from that prison. His stomach ailment was healed through prayer. His time of "facing the wall" became very special because of prayer. Yet, he had to go through the physical and emotional suffering of not knowing when or if he would ever see his family again, and he suffered much physical pain for doing nothing but carrying Bibles. Was that right? Was that just? Was it in God's plan? We have to face the fact that God's ways are not our ways, but, in His sovereignty, He knows best. This is a hard lesson for us to learn or even comprehend.

What is Prayer?

This is not an uncommon question. Prayer is not trying to persuade God to do something against His will. It is not trying to force the hand of God. It is simply being a vessel available to implement the decisions that God has already made to fulfill His plan and purpose on earth. This is ironic, considering that God does not need our help. He is sovereign and totally self-sufficient, yet He calls upon His children to pray. In the Gospel of Matthew we read: "Ask and it will be given to you; seek and you will find; knock and the door will be opened to you. For everyone who asks receives; he who seeks finds; and to him who knocks, the door is opened"

(Matthew 7:7). God *expects* us to ask Him things and to seek His face in prayer. He instructs us to knock on the door with the expectation that it will be opened. Jesus gives a very straightforward challenge when He says, "Everything is possible to him who believes" (Mark 9:23). He is also very clear when He states to His disciples, "I tell you the truth, my Father will give you whatever you ask in my name. Until now you have not asked for anything in my name. Ask and you will receive, and your joy will be complete" (John 16:23-24).

Sometimes there are conditions required to see answers to prayer. Jesus outlines those conditions in John's Gospel:

"If you remain in me and my words remain in you, ask whatever you wish, and it will be given you. This is to my Father's glory, that you bear much fruit, showing yourselves to be my disciples" (John 15:7-8).

Answers to prayer are always to bring glory to the Father. They are not just for our pleasure, convenience, or enjoyment. We do enjoy them, but that is not the end objective. Answers to prayer must bring honor and glory to God.

The Lord even gives very specific instructions to His disciples as to what they should be praying for when He says:

"The harvest is plentiful but the workers are few. Ask the Lord of the harvest therefore, to send out workers into his harvest field" (Matthew 9:37). Jesus is the Lord of the harvest, yet He instructs them to request the Lord of the harvest, Himself, to send workers out into the fields to reap the harvest. Why would He do that? The only answer is that He wants His followers to be involved and calls them to fulfill the role of workers.

There are many well known writers on the subject of prayer. The following three men made some extraordinary statements.

S.D. Gordon once said: "The greatest thing anyone can do for God and man is to pray."

E.M. Bounds said: "God shapes the world through prayer. The more praying there is in the world the better the world will be, the mightier the forces against evil."

And it was John Wesley who said: "God does nothing but in answer to prayer."

If this is true, then the Church, which is us, has an incredible responsibility to pray.

A friend sent me this story which highlights how prayer can bring about a remarkable experience of protection. I could not verify the story, but it is not dissimilar to others in such books as *Angels* by Billy Graham. It shows how responsive Christians need to be when prompted to pray for those who come to mind. It also highlights how God uses angels in His work of caring and protecting His children. The story is told by the missionary concerned, as he related it to his home church in Michigan, U.S.A.

"While serving at a small field hospital in Africa, every two weeks I traveled by bicycle through the jungle to a nearby city for supplies. This was a journey of two days and required camping overnight at the halfway point. On one of these journeys, I arrived in the city where I planned to collect money from the bank, purchase medicine and supplies, and then begin my two-day journey back to the field hospital.

"Upon my arrival in the city, I observed two men

fighting, one of whom had been seriously injured. I treated him for his injuries and at the same time talked to him about the Lord. I did what I had to do in the town and then traveled two days back home, camping overnight and arrived home without incident. I was later approached by the young man whom I had treated. He told me a remarkable and surprising account regarding the night I camped in the jungle.

"He said: 'Knowing that you were carrying money, drugs and other supplies, some friends and I followed you into the jungle, knowing you would camp overnight. We had planned to kill you and take your money and drugs. But just as we were about to move into your camp, we saw that you were surrounded by 26 armed guards.' At this I laughed, and said that I was certainly all alone in the jungle that night. The young man pressed the point, however, and said 'No sir, I was not the only person to see the guards. My friends also saw them, and we all counted them. It was because of those guards that we were afraid and left you alone.'"

As the missionary told the story to the congregation he was interrupted at this point. One man jumped to his feet and asked if the missionary could remember the exact date this happened. The missionary gave the date of the incident and the man who had interrupted replied with this story:

"On the night of your incident in Africa, it was morning here and I went out to play golf. I was about to putt when I felt the urge to pray for you. In fact, the urging of the Lord was so strong that I called men in this church to meet with me here in the sanctuary to pray for you. Would all of those men who met with me on that day stand up?" The men stood up. The missionary was not concerned with who they were, he was too busy counting how many men he saw. There were exactly 26! These were the 26 armed guards seen on the mission field!

The story is an incredible example of how the Spirit of God moves His people to pray. It highlights God involving His children in His work of protection. How important it is for us to listen and respond. If you ever hear such prodding, go along with it. Someone once said that "Nothing is ever hurt by prayer, except the gates of hell."

C.S. Lewis suggested: "all prayer is God talking to Himself."[1] The Scriptures indicate that the Holy Spirit and Jesus are interceding with the Father on our behalf; which, of course, portrays members of the Trinity communicating within the Godhead. However, there is no doubt that God involves His people in implementing His plans on earth through prayer. Our responsibility is to ensure we are available for that plan to be fulfilled.

Prayer can be very specific. For many years, a friend of ours prayed concerning the whereabouts of her children. Her estranged husband had taken them abroad and she was unable to find them. For this, she could not forgive her husband. However, she never lost the desire to know where they were, and she continued in prayer to that end. Years later, after hearing a sermon on forgiveness, she realized that she needed to extend forgiveness to her husband. Within days of doing so, she miraculously learned where her daughter was living. She had a remarkable and joyous reunion with her daughter, and ultimately with her son.

I read a similar story in one of the *Chicken Soup for the Soul* books where a man by the name of Richard Whetstone[2] also had become separated from his son in a similar fashion.

Mr. Whetstone was at the weekly prayer meeting of his church. He had quietly prayed through the list of items for prayer that week but there was still time over. So he began to pray about his son. He just wanted assurance from God as to where he was and that he was fine. He had not seen his son for many years; in fact, his son was a child the last time he saw him. Within three days, he received a letter from his estranged son, although that is not the incredible part of the story. The son had written a letter to forty-seven different Richard Whetstones and the right one received his letter three days after praying. Was this coincidence? I find it difficult to believe that such a coincidence would be so perfectly timed.

There are times we would love to see the hand of God distinctly involved as we go through the day. The reality is that we have no idea how many times God protects us, or provides for us. We don't know how often He intervenes on our behalf. We always see God's hand at work retrospectively. Just like in the "Footprints in the Sand"[3] poem, we see only one set of footprints in the sand at the times of crisis and stress in our lives. We then discover that those were the times when God was carrying us.

During the summer of 1990, I was traveling with three other pastors in Eastern Europe. We were on a four-country tour of mission projects. One morning as we left Vienna to head off into Hungary, we prayed together as a group. I remember praying very specifically that we might see God's hand upon us that day; asking that by the end of the day we would be able to know that God was intervening on our behalf. That prayer was answered in several distinct events throughout the day, two of which were outstanding.

One of the occasions occurred when we were saved from our car going over a very steep embankment at the site of an accident. Later in the day God placed it upon the heart of the pastor, whom we were due to meet in Budapest, to return home from his church. He did not know why, but we were waiting at his home. He was expecting us to meet him at the church, but we had no idea where the church was in the large city of Budapest. Hence God brought us together for ministry that evening.

God is always available to His children. We are given free access to the Father, through the Son and the Holy Spirit (Ephesians 2:18). If we walk in step with the Spirit as Galatians encourages us, and we are obedient to the voice of the Spirit, then our prayers will be Spirit-directed. It would not then be presumptuous to look for the answer. For if the Spirit of God, as well as interceding for us, instructs and inspires our prayers, then our prayers come from the very heart of God. How can they *not* be answered?

The Apostle John seems to emphasize the confidence we can have in God as we approach Him in prayer when he writes: "This is the assurance we have in approaching God: that if we ask anything according to his will; he hears us. And if we know that he hears us–whatever we ask–we know that we have what we ask of him" (1 John 5:14-15). If our prayers are directed by the Spirit of God, then surely we can have confidence that they will be answered accordingly.

Does God Always Answer Prayer?

There are times our prayers are not answered, or certainly not in the way we would like them to be. I am sure you have heard it said that God always answers prayer. He either says: "Yes," "No," or "Not yet." Even if that is true, it is often hard to discern between the last two. There are places in Scripture where answers to prayers were not forthcoming. Paul's experience was an example where he definitely did not receive the answer to prayer that he had in mind. Talking about the "thorn in the flesh" that plagued him he said: "Three times I pleaded with the Lord to take it away from me. But he said to me 'My grace is sufficient for you, for my power is made perfect in weakness.' Therefore I will boast all the more gladly about my weaknesses, so that Christ's power may rest on me. That is why for Christ's sake, I delight in weaknesses, in insults, in hardships, in persecutions, in difficulties. For when I am weak, then I am strong" (2 Corinthians 12:7-10).

Daniel also wrestled with not receiving an immediate answer to his prayer; although he learned later that his prayer was actually answered at the moment it was uttered. It was three weeks later that he received the answer personally (Daniel 10:12-13). The answer had been delayed by demonic forces. How many of our prayers for loved ones and others are being delayed by such forces? The prayer of faith binds the Devil and his forces. This certainly was not one of those incidences where God was saying, "Not yet!" Daniel's prayer received an immediate answer but the answer disturbed the opposition, hence the delay. The only effective power in defeating Satan is the power of the Holy Spirit, which is released and becomes effective by the prayers of God's people.

However, there are other reasons for unanswered prayer. James talks about this in his epistle. He suggests that prayerlessness and selfish intentions may be the problem. He states: "You do not have, because you do not ask God. When you ask, you do not receive, because you ask with the wrong motives" (James 4:2-3). Obviously we cannot see God's answers to prayer if we do not pray. But when we do pray, what are our motives? Are those motives ultimately for the glory of God or are we seeking answers for our own benefit and convenience? However, it is difficult to understand why when we do pray with the right motives; for instance for the blessing of others and for the glory of God, we sometimes still receive no answer. It is at those times that we have no recourse but to be thrust back on the sovereignty of God, on His faithfulness, and to our ongoing relationship with Him as His child.

Later in his letter, James talks about the "prayer of faith." Do we exercise faith? When we pray do we expect things to remain the same? Do we subscribe to the thinking that we should pray about everything, but all the while thinking: "Whatever will be, will be?" Is this not fatalism?

This, of course, is in direct opposition to the words of Jesus when He said: "I tell you the truth, anyone who has faith in me will do what I have been doing. He will do even greater things than these, because I am going to the Father. And I will do whatever you ask in my name, so that the Son may bring glory to the Father. You may ask me for anything in my name, and I will do it" (John 14:12-14). I believe faith is a gift which, if planted in the heart by the Holy Spirit, will result in the implementation of the will of God. I believe God wants us, as His children, to be involved in that which He wishes to achieve on earth. For that we need to be sensitive to the Spirit of God, including what He might want to achieve through the prayers of us, His children.

It is easy to say that "God knows best," but that is little comfort for those going through a serious loss or heartache. It is true that many lessons have been learned because God did not answer our prayer, or did not grant us the answer for which we asked. However, there are times when we have no option but to yield to the sovereignty of God, which means that He rules over all and is in control. His plans cannot be thwarted. We yield to His greater knowledge and understanding. We think we know best and know what would be best for us, but we have to admit that there have been times when that has not proven to be the case. Sometimes we experience untold concern and stress when adverse events happen and doors close on us, only to find that God eventually overcomes the situation or simply opens another door.

We have concentrated only on one side of prayer, that of supplication. That is because we have only been looking at the question, "Does God answer prayer?" However, we should not overlook that prayer involves much more than just presenting our requests. It must include our worship, devotion, praise, and thanksgiving. We must come into the presence of God in the right attitude; confessing our sin and seeking His forgiveness. We have no rights per se to present anything to God except through the finished work of Christ on Calvary. It is only through Him that we are invited into the throne room of God to offer our praise along with our petitions. God delights in the praises of His people. Because God is just, He will forgive us our sin when we confess. The Psalmist assures us that He hears us when we cry to Him

(Psalm 40:1). He provides for us when we need it. He delivers us from crises. He is the Sovereign Lord and He is in control. Because He is infinite, He already knows what we are going through and what we will go through in the days ahead.

We can take comfort and consolation from the fact that even when we do not immediately see the answer to our prayer, we can still trust God implicitly. God has already been where we are and He promises to be there with us always. One day we will understand why some of our prayers were answered, while seemingly others were not. We bow to God's authority and defer to His wisdom in all things and in all situations. We must rest in the assurance that He really does know best.

GUIDE FOR GROUP STUDY

Chapter 2: Does God Answer Prayer?

Bible reading: Luke 18:1-8

1 Then Jesus told his disciples a parable to show them that they should always pray and not give up. 2 He said: "In a certain town there was a judge who neither feared God nor cared what people thought. 3 And there was a widow in that town who kept coming to him with the plea, 'Grant me justice against my adversary.'

4 "For some time he refused. But finally he said to himself, 'Even though I don't fear God or care what people think, 5 yet because this widow keeps bothering me, I will see that she gets justice, so that she won't eventually come and attack me!'"

6 And the Lord said, "Listen to what the unjust judge says. 7 And will not God bring about justice for his chosen ones, who cry out to him day and night? Will he keep putting them off? 8 I tell you, he will see that they get justice, and quickly. However, when the Son of Man comes, will he find faith on the earth?"

Questions for discussion:

1) Share your own experience of answered prayer. Share stories of others you know who also have received answers to prayer.

2) How does God answer prayer?

3) Do you believe God <u>always</u> answers prayer? What support do you have for your answer?

4) What role does faith play in God answering prayer? Can you biblically support your answer?

5) Can a person pray with a wrong motive? What motive should a person have in prayer?

6) Is there benefit in praying with non-believers?

CHAPTER THREE:
DOES GOD HEAL?

"... for I am the Lord who heals you."

Exodus 15:26

It was in 1986 that, for the second time, my wife discovered a lump in her breast. The first one three years previously had been benign, so we immediately concluded that this would probably be the same. We were wrong. The biopsy and the mammogram indicated cancer. We did not know these results until we arrived at the hospital for my wife to have what we thought was a routine removal of a benign tumor. She was in for a three day hospital stay. She was duly admitted and the nurse said, "Mrs. Murray, your room is down there on the left and, Mr. Murray, the doctor wishes to speak with you." I thought that was rather ominous.

The doctor was elsewhere in the hospital and talked to me on the telephone. His words were devastating.

"John, I am sorry to tell you that your wife has cancer

and you will need to sign a form giving us permission to do more surgery, possibly a mastectomy!"

It was difficult to reply. In fact, I cannot remember what my reply was. Then he said, "You will have to go and tell Rita, I will come by to see you in a while." I immediately went and sat down for a few moments to recover from the shock, and to consider how best to break the news to my wife. What they were proposing was not somewhere in the future, but the next morning!

It was not difficult for my wife to realize that something was amiss. I broke the unwelcome news to her but added, "We are going to pray for your healing."

It was not long before the doctor came in, who then explained the laboratory report on the biopsy. It showed definite cancer cells. I asked what the mammogram had shown and he said that it was a dark area at the point of the tumor and this, he said, was significant in these cases.

My answer to him astonished myself. I said, "Well, whatever the lab report says and whatever the mammogram shows, I believe God will heal my wife before you operate tomorrow morning!" Then I thought, *What have I just said?*

The doctor replied, "Well, let's just take one thing at a time."

I said that I would only sign the form for a lumpectomy. He concurred with my decision and left with the form signed accordingly.

My wife and I immediately prayed together. It was a simple prayer asking for God's healing, not just for our benefit, but that it would be a witness and testimony to God's healing power and His grace. We wanted it as a blessing and an encouragement to others to whom we ministered at that time. Then we began calling people on the telephone right from the hospital room. We asked people to stand with us in prayer, and that we were praying for my wife to be healed before they operated in the morning. The request was met with varying reactions. Some people were excited and positively wanted to join in praying with us. Others agreed, but with a little less enthusiasm.

One particular pastor insisted on praying for the will of God, rather than to ask for a specific healing.

By late in the evening, we estimated that about fifty people had joined us in our prayer request for my wife's healing. I went home and prayed with my son before going to bed. I awoke early and spent some more time in prayer. Around 7:00 a.m., I was on my knees praying when this came into my mind: "She will not need the extra surgery!"

I cannot say that it was an audible voice, but it was a very definite impression on my mind which led me to say, "Thank you Father, that's all I needed to know." I asked God for a verse of Scripture that would confirm what was taking place. He gave me: "Before they call, I will answer and while they yet speak, I will hear" (Isaiah 65:24). This truth became even more significant when I learned that there were people meeting to pray for my wife during the time of the operation.

Because visiting time was not until afternoon, I went off to work and at 10:30 a.m. the telephone rang. It was the surgeon on the phone who said, "John, we can find no cancer whatsoever!"

I shouted, "Praise the Lord!" so loud that people came from other offices to see what was happening. I called the group who were praying at that time–the prayer meeting turned into a praise meeting! Ringing in my mind was: "What a great God we serve!" Rita came home a couple of days later. Her story has been a testimony to God's healing power. It has been a witness to His goodness and His grace.

We have a friend who, not long ago, had a rather nasty fall. A bone in her hand was broken and her hip was injured. She received medical treatment for the broken hand and it was suggested that the hip was just sprained and would be right again in a few days. She left the hospital with her hand in a cast. For the next ten days she continued walking, although the hip was painful and far from right. Another x-ray was arranged, the result of which showed that the hip was actually broken. At the time, she was attending an Alpha program at her church, so it was natural for the leaders of Alpha to have special prayer for her healing. This was followed by her pastor and the elders of the church praying for her and anointing her with oil. After prayer, on her way home she suffered excruciating pain, both in her hip and in the hand.

Later, the hospital called regarding possible surgery for the hip. In preparation for the procedure, her hip was x-rayed once again. Looking at the x-rays, the surgeon indicated that surgery was not needed because it seemed to be miraculously healing; the hand had also healed. Surprised by this, the doctors insisted that further x-rays and a check-up be made every two weeks. Each time, the hip was better than before. The medical staff were amazed at the results, considering the normal time it takes for a hip to heal. Our friend then went on a previously planned holiday to Ireland and Scotland. She did take one crutch with her, just in case it was needed, and to give the hip some respite from the strenuous walking and climbing of castle stairs on the trip. She had no problems.

Oddly enough, the only other attack of pain was when she was requested to share her healing testimony with the church. The pain returned just before her public witness. However, once it was over, there was no reoccurrence of pain. She now walks completely without any discomfort and is grateful to God for the complete healing she enjoyed.

Long term illness is something else. It is debilitating, both mentally and physically. It brings discouragement and loneliness. Regardless of what kind of disease it is, the whole experience can be depressing, especially if there is no relief of the physical pain and mental anguish. Hopelessness is an accompanying emotion.

Probably one of the most disconcerting aspects of illness is feeling that you are no longer in control. It can bring fear and even panic. We have a deep desire to be in control at all times, but regrettably that is not always possible when illness comes upon us. We become dependent upon doctors, nurses, friends, and relatives from whom we derive support. We have a very close friend who has had a very severe struggle with cancer. It was thought to be terminal. He had to return from the mission field because of his illness. He had a serious operation, spent months recovering, has had a second onslaught of the disease, and is left with inoperable internal tumours, which are under constant observation. He wrote the following words which applied to this situation because he felt that, in the turmoil of his illness, he was losing control. These were his words;

"Whenever I feel panic, fear, or depression, it is often a sign that I am counting on my own limited and undependable resources or at least on other insufficient and unreliable human resources, rather than on God. I need to learn how to disengage this 'auto-response' or 'default mode' which seeks refuge, solace, or solutions solely in my own resources. I need to train my heart into the habit of turning to God in dependence and trust; no matter what comes my way. God alone is my ultimate resource and my refuge of absolute security. That's where I want to be."

What an incredible aspiration! Not easy to put into practice, but it certainly is where we, as Christians, should seek to be. Carmen Benson, who wrote a book entitled *What About Those of Us Who Are Not Healed?* writes, "God has not abandoned us. His purpose in allowing suffering is not to get us down. His purpose is to build us up. He has something better for us. If healing was for our greatest good, the Lord would heal us. He is molding us, reshaping us, to conform us to the likeness of Christ, and that often entails suffering."[1]

Does God Always Heal?

Does God always heal? No! In fact we have to recognize that more people are not healed than are healed. Why is this? We do not know. What we do know, is that all things work according to God's sovereignty. Sometimes He heals for His glory, and another time He does not heal, also for His glory. Either way, the end result is that He receives the glory.

It is not easy to accept when we are among those who are not healed. As a young man, I saw my own mother healed of arthritis in the hip. She had difficulty walking to the front of the church where elders laid hands on her, anointing her with oil. After the prayer she walked away, totally upright, totally free of pain and suffered no more with arthritis in her hip. Yet I have seen many others prayed for in exactly the same way and nothing has changed.

Carmen Benson speaks directly from experience when she says, "Regardless of the cause, regardless of the cures, He is sovereign. He runs the universe His way and according to His timing. He has His reasons for intervening in the lives of those who receive miracles of healing; He has His reasons for withholding healing intervention in the lives of those whom He does not heal."[2]

She is right. God is sovereign. A fact that is hard to acknowledge when dealing with our own suffering.

People who suffer are certainly given the right to speak on the issue. Benson, who suffered incredibly with many physical ailments, asked this question of the Lord: "Your ears seem deaf to my pleas as well as to the pleas of others in my behalf. Why is this, dear Lord?"

The reply she received was, "My ears are not deaf to the cries of my children, nor is my arm powerless to deliver. Because I do not answer as you desire does not mean I am unmindful or unheeding. My ways are not your ways and my timing is not regulated according to the will of man."[3]

It is remarkable to think that if Job had not suffered as he did, the book of Job would not have been written. We would never have learned from his incredible faithfulness to God. As it is, there are few people in the Western world, inside and outside the Church, who have not heard of Job's sufferings and his patience. Yet, God did not give Job a reason for his suffering. Is God obligated to provide us with an answer to the questions: "Why me?" or "Why this?" or even the question of "How long, Lord, do I go on suffering?"

It is not uncommon for us to look for reasons for our

suffering, but often we look in the wrong direction for those reasons and ask the wrong questions. We tend to ask, "What did I do wrong?" or "What sin did I commit that brought this about?"

Questions like these are quite natural, but usually they are irrelevant because God does not work that way. This is not to dismiss the fact that some have suffered because of sin, but it is not a normal situation. Our sin was totally dealt with at the cross. We live in a completely forgiven state. God does not bring judgment upon His children in the form of disease. Misconceptions like these can cause us added emotional and spiritual stress. When asked by His disciples about the illness of one man as to whether he or his parents had sinned, Jesus replied that it was neither he nor his parents who had sinned, but that God should be glorified. God can, and should, be glorified whether we are miraculously healed or healed through the expertise of the medical profession. All healing comes from God.

Over twenty years ago, I had cancer which was not miraculously healed. The tumor was removed and everything was fine, but the experience taught me many different spiritual lessons, not least of which was the value and strength received by those who were faithful in prayer. One busy pastor called on the telephone every morning at 8:00 a.m. to pray with me until the ordeal was over. He and I shared communion together alone in his church, at which time he prayed especially for a miracle of healing. It was he who took me to the hospital, and it was he who was there when I returned home. I learned much through that experience about faithfulness in caring, and the spiritual support which comes through praying for a friend.

For about twenty-five years we have been friends with a couple, who, while working devotedly in service for the Kingdom, were put through an excruciating period of suffering. Emigrating from what was then Yugoslavia to Canada was no small decision, but they were young and saw the opportunity for progress and the possibility of "making it" in the new country. Things went well. The husband eventually owned his own watch-repair business and his wife had her own dental laboratory. However, after eight years in Canada they felt God would have them return to their own country and share the good news of the Christian faith. They did just that, but things then did not go well.

There was no response from those whom they tried to reach with the Gospel and no encouragement from the local churches. Then, the wife had a baby and from day one, she knew there was something wrong with her new son, Filip. Doctors had difficulty diagnosing any real problem with his health, but made various suggestions as to what the problem might be. Most of their suggestions were illnesses that the child would have to live with and endure, however, at his six month check up, the doctors found something drastically wrong. They took x-rays and discovered tumors on both kidneys.

The news was devastating, and even more so when the doctors indicated that there was nothing they could do for their son in Serbia. Their advice was, "Catch the first flight back to Canada. There's no time to sell the house. You must seek help immediately."

The airline officials cooperated, and booked them on an already overbooked flight under emergency provisions. Within a day or so, they were back in Canada.

Arriving in Canada, they went straight to the hospital. They had been away from Canada for more than a year, but miraculously their insurance was reinstated with the coverage commencing immediately with no premiums to pay. They could not believe it. It was just one of the many miracles God provided at the time. Others occurred as the days went by: a place to stay, a loaned car, clothes, and household items. God was taking care of the details. But then came the worst possible news from the hospital. The doctors told them that Filip was in the advanced stage of cancer in both kidneys. There was no other case like it in Canada, and only thirty cases had ever been recorded. None of the children had survived.

Thinking back on their situation, it did not take the couple long to realize that it was during the critical stage of the pregnancy that the Chernobyl nuclear reactor exploded. As the prevailing winds carried the toxic radioactive dust into Yugoslavia, it was determined that their picnicking in the countryside at that time caused the exposure to the deadly poison. Naturally, as Christians, questions began to flood their minds. Why did they go back? Why did God allow the pregnancy at that time? Did they not go to serve God? Were they not there to share the Gospel with others for the sake of the Kingdom? Did they really hear from God in the first place, instructing them to return to their homeland? They had many questions, but no answers.

The doctors operated on Filip but closed him up again, because the tumor on one kidney was so large that it would have been too dangerous to take it out. He would not have survived. He was immediately put on chemotherapy treatment in order to reduce the tumors so that they might be removed. The treatment was extremely hard on him. The chemotherapy had a detrimental effect on the rest of his body. It was hard for his parents to watch him. He rarely smiled and did not have the strength to cry.

It was decided to remove one kidney. Six months had now passed and the time came for the operation. The couple asked the elders of their church to come and pray for their son. They prayed and their church prayed. They expected the operation to go well and expected to hear that the cancer had gone from the other kidney. After it was over the news was still not good. The doctors had removed the kidney with the largest tumor, but the other kidney was still cancerous. The chemotherapy was increased to the largest possible dosage for a child of his age. His suffering was immense and devastatingly hard for his mother to take, especially as she stayed at the hospital night and day with Filip. However, the nightmare was about to get worse.

A doctor mistakenly administered concentrated potassium to their son and within minutes, he was in cardiac arrest. A hospital emergency crew was there in seconds, and after some while, they were able to revive him; but now the question loomed, "Did he suffer brain damage?" Filip was put into the intensive care unit and hooked up to an even more hideous number of tubes. More questions came to mind. Why was this happening? Why were they going through such agony? Had God forgotten them? Had He abandoned them at this crucial time?

The second, more severe round of chemotherapy treatment did not impact the cancer on the other kidney. It had been fifteen months since their arrival back in Canada. They were absolutely exhausted and at the point of total distress. More surgery was planned within three weeks. This time, it would be to remove whatever cancer they could, just in an effort to extend the child's life. Hope had virtually disappeared.

It was at this juncture that the couple went to a Sunday service at the church they attended and asked the elders to anoint their son and pray for him again. In the words of his mother, "Something unusual happened in my heart as we walked up the aisle for prayer. Those few steps made a huge difference in my heart. I knew God had compassion. I knew that He understood how I felt. But as I walked, I said to God, 'You can have him.' Every time I had prayed before, while I was in the hospital, while I watched him dying, while I watched him go through this agony, I had prayed, 'Do whatever you want with Filip, but please don't let him die.' I had given God a condition. Now, for the first time, I meant it when I told God that He could have Filip. I wasn't angry at God. I was just so tired. I said, 'God, either heal him or take him.' It seemed so simple. I had two other children who needed me. And I thought, 'If Filip has to go through more agony and pain and is going to die anyway, then, Lord, you can take him.'"

Nothing spectacular happened after the prayer except that the husband immediately said to his wife, "I believe he's healed."

The wife could not readily agree at that point. An elderly man came up to them whom they had never seen before. He asked to hold their son. He held Filip and simply exclaimed, "Your son is healed. All you have to do is give God the glory now and praise Him for his healing."

The husband replied, "Well, the surgery is in ten days.

Can we contact you to let you know?"

The man answered, "No, you can't because I'm moving." They never saw the man again. They always wondered if he was one of God's angels.

The time for the surgery came. Filip was wheeled down to the operating room and the parents waited. It was an anxious time as they sat and waited and waited. The minutes seemed like hours. They had expected to hear from a nurse as to how the surgery was going, but no one came out to talk with them at all. They were convinced something had gone wrong. Then after more than three hours the surgeon came out himself. This was most unusual and unexpected. They feared the worst.

They will never forget the words of the surgeon. He said, "There is nothing there. We cannot see any trace of cancer. We took over thirty-five biopsies of the liver, bowels and the kidney, as well as a number of spots on the kidney."

Something miraculous had taken place in Filip's little body. In two days he recovered. They were able to take him from the hospital, never to return again. God had healed him before he reached his second birthday. But God not only healed him, He kept him from all the potential adverse side effects from the heavy drugs. He preserved him from the brain damage which could have resulted from the heart attack.

His mother said, "Filip is a miracle of God, but so am I, his mother, as well as his father and sisters. Many miracles took place and all the glory goes to God. We faced an agonizing time in our life, not knowing that it was all part of God's perfect plan."[4]

God did not abandon them. God did not forget them.

God brought them through the valley of despair, the valley of death. Filip is now a strong robust young man and, looking at him today, nobody could ever imagine the events covering the first two years of his life.

What is God Teaching Us?

As already mentioned, more people are not healed than healed, which provides little comfort to those who continue in their suffering. If we are among those who have to wait indefinitely for our healing, or if we are not healed at all, what do we learn from it? We certainly learn patience and endurance. We also learn to have compassion and understanding for others. For us, personally, it is always a period of testing, of purifying and maybe a time of maturing spiritually. Who knows, perhaps if we were to receive complete healing, we might then be too busy to give attention to the Lord and to our spiritual condition.

Although it is difficult, it is certainly good if we can identify with Paul when he says in Romans, "...but we also rejoice in our sufferings, because we know that suffering produces perseverance; perseverance, character; and character, hope. And hope does not disappoint us, because God has poured out his love into our hearts by the Holy Spirit, whom he has given us" (Romans 5:3-5).

Knowing what we know, we do not question God's *ability* to heal, but we do question *why* He does not heal when we ask Him. As I write these words, my wife is suffering from an exhausting and debilitating illness. Night and day, for a long time, we have prayed for her healing. The heavens seem closed. We seem to hear nothing but silence. From the past experience of her being healed we wonder,

Why not this time? Our spiritual experience, our spiritual knowledge and understanding remind us of the truth that God is the same yesterday, today, and forever (Hebrews 13:8). That same understanding tells us that God does hear, that God does answer prayer, that God does love His children unconditionally and is concerned about the smallest things in their lives. Yet we continue to look for the outward evidence that He is acting on those biblical principles.

We are still left with the unanswered question of "why?" Ready answers are not always available. We ask God for patience. We ask Him what it is that He wants to teach us in this situation, in the belief that He is shaping us into a vessel to be used in His service. Neither is it easy for us to sit back and simply accept the truth of Scripture when it says, "...his ways are past finding out" (Romans 11:33 AV).

Paul could speak from experience. The Scripture says that to keep him from becoming conceited after experiencing an incredible vision, he was given "a thorn in the flesh." We are not told exactly what it was, but obviously it was some physical weakness, illness, or disability. Three times he asked for it to be removed and three times the answer was in the negative. It appears that Paul was refused his request for healing so that his ego would not be satisfied.

Knowing what we know about Paul's writings, it's hard to imagine, but maybe his pride would have been a problem. Pride can be an obstacle in receiving answered prayers, primarily because of how we might handle the answer. God will not share His glory. God's answer to Paul in his circumstances was simply, "My grace is sufficient for you, for my power is made perfect in weakness" (2 Corinthians 12:7).

Paul then said that he would boast in his weaknesses because they gave opportunity for God's strength to be recognized. He confidently says, "I consider that our present sufferings are not worth comparing with the glory that will be revealed in us" (Romans 8:18), as he looks forward to the ultimate end of all suffering. He looks to the time when God "will wipe every tear from their eyes. There will be no more death or mourning or crying or pain, for the old order of things has passed away" (Revelations 21:4).

The Scriptures are replete with examples of God's hand of healing. From the book of Exodus, God informs the children of Israel that, "I am the Lord who heals you" (Exodus 15:26). However, the promise of healing for them held the conditions of listening to God's voice, obeying His commands, and putting His decrees into operation. Many others were blessed with healing in the Old Testament including Naaman, healed of leprosy (2 Kings 5:14) and Hezekiah, who was granted another fifteen years of life (Isaiah 28).

In the New Testament also we are left with many examples of healing through the ministry of Jesus (Matthew 4:23) and then through the apostles in the book of Acts. It seemed that, at that time, healing was a regular occurrence accompanying the preaching of God's Word. Obviously, we are delighted because it did not stop there. God still heals today. But He does not heal at man's demand, or simply upon request. God heals as *He* wills, in *His* time, according to *His* plan, according to *His* purpose and especially, in accordance with *His* divine sovereignty.

GUIDE FOR GROUP STUDY

Chapter 3: Does God Heal?

Bible reading: Matthew 9:35-38

35 Jesus went through all the towns and villages, teaching in their synagogues, proclaiming the good news of the kingdom and healing every disease and sickness.
36 When he saw the crowds, he had compassion on them, because they were harassed and helpless, like sheep without a shepherd.
37 Then he said to his disciples, "The harvest is plentiful but the workers are few. 38 Ask the Lord of the harvest, therefore, to send out workers into his harvest field."

Questions for discussion:

1) Have you, or anyone close to you, ever received a miracle of healing from God? Explain the situation.

2) If you believe that God heals today, in what way(s) does He do this?

3) As God's children, do we have a right to be healed? What Scripture might support your answer?

4) Should we always pray for God's healing? Why or why not?

5) How does the sovereignty of God fit into His healing activity?

6) Do we or can we know what hinders healing in our lives?

7) For what purpose might God withhold healing from us?

8) How should we handle the situation when we are not healed?

CHAPTER FOUR:
DOES GOD GUIDE?

"For I know the plans I have for you," declares the Lord, "plans to prosper you and not to harm you, plans to give you a hope and a future."

Jeremiah 29:11

Being followed by the Secret Police or a government appointed spy is rather disarming. Yet for the visitor in Eastern Europe during the communist era, this was a common experience. As a foreigner in communist countries, it was generally unwise to ask for directions, because it would often be reported to the authorities as to where you were going. You were followed, so authorities could discover who you were planning to meet.

Every Christian is keen to know God's guidance but, in Eastern Europe at that time, it was a complete necessity. The danger for resident believers was far greater than for visitors. Visitors could easily be deported, but resident Christians had to stay to face the oppression and consequences. Was it coincidental that visiting Christians had found that "accidentally" they were in the right place at the right time, where they met "by chance" the very people they were seeking?

In his book *Questions of Life*, which is a written version of the Alpha video tapes, Nicky Gumbel relates one such story. Talking about guidance from God, he says, "Sometimes He opens doors in a remarkable way. The circumstances and the timing point clearly to the hand of God."

He goes on to relate this story: "Michael Bordeaux is head of Keston College, a research unit devoted to helping believers in what were communist lands. His work and research are respected by governments all over the world. He studied Russian at Oxford. His Russian teacher, Dr. Zernov, sent him a letter which he had received, because he thought it would interest him. It detailed how monks were being beaten up by the KGB and subjected to inhuman medical examinations; how they were being rounded up in lorries (trucks) and dumped many hundreds of miles away. The letter was written very simply, with no adornment, and as he read it Michael Bordeaux felt he was hearing the true voice of the persecuted Church. The letter was signed Varavva and Pronina.

"In August 1964 he went on a trip to Moscow, and on his first evening there he met up with old friends who detailed how the persecutions were getting worse; in particular the old church of St. Peter and St. Paul had been demolished. They suggested that he go and see it for himself.

"So he took a taxi, arriving at dusk. When he came to the square where he had remembered a very beautiful church, he found nothing except a twelve-foot-high fence which hid the rubble where the church had been. Over on the other side of the square, climbing the fence to try to see what was inside, were two women. He watched them, and when they finally left the square he followed them for a hundred yards and eventually caught them up.

"They asked, 'Who are you?'

"He replied 'I am a foreigner. I have come to find out what is happening here in the Soviet Union.'

"They took him back to the house of another woman who asked why he had come. Whereupon he said he had received a letter from the Ukraine via Paris. When she asked who it was from, he replied, 'Varavva and Pronina.' There was silence. He wondered if he had said something wrong. There followed a flood of uncontrolled sobbing. The woman pointed and said, 'This is Varavva and this is Pronina.'

"The population of Russia is over 140 million. The Ukraine, from where the letter was written, is 1300 kilometres from Moscow. Michael Bordeaux had flown from England six months after the letter had been written. They would not have met had either party arrived at the demolished church an hour earlier or an hour later. That was one of the ways God called Michael Bordeaux to set up his life's work."[1]

Obedience Precedes Guidance

God's guidance comes to us in different ways. Sometimes we are unsure as to why certain doors open and others close. It is interesting that Paul would stay on in Ephesus "because a great door for effective work has opened to me, and there are many who oppose me" (1 Corinthians 16:9). One would imagine that opposition would indicate that it was time to leave. He recognized the door which God had opened and he knew his responsibility was to stay on the job until God moved him on. Sometimes we are guided by God without even being aware of it. We need to be obedient to what is immediately before us, and then God will reveal His ultimate plan and purpose. Such was the case on my first visit to Moscow.

Within 24 hours of arriving in Moscow, I found myself in prison. It was not because I had entered Russia with contraband or even Bibles. It was no mistake, it had been planned. We had received an invitation from a prison Commandant to visit his prison for a day. We had no idea he had an ulterior motive.

The prison, at Egorevsk, about 120 kilometres south of Moscow, was a maximum security prison. It was difficult for us to get in, so it was probably even more difficult for prisoners to get out. We went through several doors, and each one locked behind us. Finally inside, we were welcomed by the Commandant who invited us to look around. He gave us total freedom to enter any cell if we wished to speak with the inmates. There were 1,500 prisoners inside those four walls.

We spent from 10:30 in the morning until 3:30 in the afternoon at the prison. After being shown around, we took the opportunity of having the guards unlock some cells for us so that not only could we talk with the prisoners, but we could also see the conditions of their accommodation. The conditions in which they survived were nothing short of atrocious. We spent some time locked in the cells with the prisoners.

The cell doors were made of steel with a lock and several bolts on the outside. At eye level there was a small opening used by the guards to keep watch, but also large enough to pass through a dish of soup. Inside the cells the walls and the floor were stark cold concrete. There were bunk beds enough to sleep six men. However, the cell was home to fifteen men. We were told that there were other cells to accommodate 20 which housed 50 men. Apparently the strongest got the beds, the rest slept on the floor. Their washing facility was a small hand wash basin with cold running water. The basin was absolutely filthy, covered with grime. Their toilet was simply a hole in the concrete floor in one corner of the cell. It was summer, so the smell in this crowded room was nauseating.

We spent quite some time with the men sharing the Christian faith before we moved on to others. Right next to the first cell was another, occupied this time by women. The cell was the same size and identical in facilities, but this time there were only about ten inmates. Most of the women were in prison for murder and usually the murder of a spouse or family members. We were told that the consumption of alcohol had a great deal to do with the crimes committed. The women were very attentive to our message and grateful for prayer. A number of them were in tears, especially those who had been brought up in the traditions of the Russian Orthodox Church.

The surprise came at the end of our visit. We were invited to the office of the Commandant where we were given tea and cake. Then the announcement came from our host, "I should have told you this before" he said, "but at least 50% of our prisoners have TB!" We had spent a day in close contact with these inmates and now we learned that at least half of them had tuberculosis. It was somewhat of a surprise. He went on, "I invited you here and allowed you to speak to the prisoners simply because I need your help. You see, I desperately need medicine for these TB patients. I cannot obtain it anywhere. Even the government or medical people here cannot provide it for us. I was wondering whether you people from the West could help us. I would be most grateful if you could."

We were able to help. The necessary medicine was purchased in the West and shipped to our co-workers in Russia who, in turn, made the delivery to the prison. The Commandant naturally was delighted. The result of our visit was that the prison became an open mission field. Our co-workers were allowed in to share the Gospel on a regular basis.

Commenced at the same time was a ministry to rehabilitate prisoners upon their release. In Russia, an ex-prisoner had to receive permission from the local police superintendent before he or she could reside in any chosen town or jurisdiction. Consequently, most were not wanted or welcomed anywhere which caused further problems of homelessness. This rehabilitation ministry was established to help them find a place to live and a place to work. In fact, a 3,000 hectare farm was used to provide work for these men with local accommodation available.

Today, a small church exists there where over 30 ex-prisoners worship, all of whom have come to faith in Christ since being released from prison. We had no idea what God had in mind when we accepted the invitation to visit that prison. Does God guide? It certainly would appear that it was no accident the way events fell into place, providing long-term overall spiritual benefit for the prison inmates.

There is a real danger for us to talk too glibly about the guidance of God. It is not uncommon to think that we can just "put out a fleece" as Gideon did and God will respond. Had God not already promised Gideon victory (Judges 6:36)? Had He not already spoken to Gideon as to what he must do, before Gideon put out the fleece for confirmation? God has given us basic lessons in guidance through His Word. He has left us some specific guidelines as to what is right and wrong regarding His moral law. If we are looking for guidance on a matter which diametrically opposes God's law, then the word has already been given. In addition to His Word, He has given us intelligence and a sense of responsibility. As God has given it to us, I am sure He expects us to use it. Therefore, we should act responsibly when it comes to matters of guidance. That is not to say, of course, there are situations where we need to hear specific guidance from God, regarding a certain issue or to know the way forward.

Guidance in Everyday Issues

If we are looking for guidance in our everyday decisions, we have to ask the question, "Is this something I can decide or does it require a direct word from God?" We must never overlook that the believer is indwelt by the Spirit of God who, Jesus said, "would guide us into all truth" (John 16:13). I know this is normally interpreted as relating to the truth of Scripture and that is correct, but decisions we make must be influenced by the Spirit living within, if we live in submission to Him. As the Spirit of God is part of the Godhead, we can expect the guidance we need to be given by

Him. Even when we pray to the Father seeking His wisdom and guidance, the answer arrives through the voice and presence of the Holy Spirit.

Asking for guidance is always fraught with potential danger; one of which is seeking to get God's stamp of approval on the plans of our choice. We make up our minds as to which way we want to go and then ask God to put His seal upon it. There is nothing wrong with seeking God's confirmation to ensure that we are on the right track, as long as we are not doing things of our own choice, seeking His blessing on it and then saying, "God told me to do it."

We are instructed to commit our way to the Lord and to fully trust Him (Psalm 37:5). This is a prerequisite before we can expect God to give us specific guidance. We also read that, "He guides the humble in what is right and teaches them his way. All the ways of the Lord are loving and faithful for those who keep the demands of his covenant" (Psalm 25:9-10). We learn from this Psalm that having humility and the right attitude is required from us to hear from God. We need to be people who are open and willing to do what God calls us to do. We do not have the right to demand of God or dictate to God. We must not come to God with our own agenda. However, one major blessing for us is that we know that His ways are loving and faithful. This gives us comfort and confidence that His direction will result in what is best for us.

There is another condition mentioned in this scripture that is required of us if we are to be a recipient of this blessing. We must "keep the demands of his covenant." How do we do that, especially as it relates to seeking guidance? It requires that we walk in step with the Spirit, so that our lives receive the direction of the Spirit of God. We read elsewhere that "...those who live in accordance with the Spirit have their minds set on what the Spirit desires"(Romans 8:7). If we know what the Spirit desires, then surely we know the mind of God?

How many times have you heard the phrase, "The Lord led me"? This is easy to say but hard to prove or disprove. I knew a gentleman who owned a store. He sold the store saying that the Lord "led him" to do so. Nine months later, he bought the store back again. He did not say he had received divine guidance to buy it back. But who made the mistake, the Lord or the store owner? Maybe there was a legitimate reason why he needed to sell the store. It appeared that he bought it back because the new owner could not make a success of it. However, to the outsider, his action would seem somewhat incongruous as he insisted that he had received guidance from God. Maybe it was unnecessary to bring the Lord into it at all.

When it comes to seeking guidance for jobs and places to live, there is a divergence of opinion. It is right that we pray about all things in our lives, particularly about major moves and life-altering changes, but then the question is raised, "Is God concerned about where we live or what we do for a living?" We like to think so, but does that preclude any freedom we might have to choose our occupation or even the place we call home? There are certainly instances where God has distinctly called a person and placed them in a particular location or position, and has used them extensively to be a blessing to others. There are others, however, who have moved into a new community out of choice, or for employment reasons without seeking specific divine guidance, and God has also used them to be an incredible blessing in their new location. This then raises the question as to whether God placed them or simply used them once they were there. Does God actually guide us into all situations or does He use the circumstances and the situation for His glory, according to our willingness to be used? I believe God does both.

Is not our personal relationship with God more important than our choice of livelihood? Is not our walk with God more important than our choice of where we live? What about the house we buy or the car we drive; do we exercise any freedom of choice in these matters? God can always use us where we are and with whatever we have to give Him. The essential aspect is a willingness to be used for His glory. Some people like to think that God gives guidance on every issue in life, however great or small. If this is the case for you, then that is wonderful, but one cannot help wondering whether or not God would require consultation upon all the menial daily tasks of life.

God is interested in our lives, thus, whatever we do, however insignificant, we must do it for Him and for His glory. We must never overlook the fact that the Holy Spirit is resident in the life of the Christian for the very purpose of guidance. If we are not careful, we can make the Holy Spirit redundant in our lives, because it is He who gives us direction and discernment as to how we should conduct our lives, including our everyday activity. Paul emphasizes that as we live in the Spirit so we shall be led by the Spirit (Romans 8:14).

Does not the permissive will of God, and the particular will of God, come into play regarding guidance? Are there not situations in which God allows us to make our own decisions, while in others, He specifically gives us direction because of a particular task He has for us to do? I think this is the case. We pray about all things, allowing God in His sovereignty to determine where and when we need this specific guidance. Sometimes God's very provision can also be His guidance.

There is no question that God gives very special guidance and provision in particular situations. I think of the communist governments and their restrictions in not allowing the free movement of their own people around the country. It was even more difficult for foreigners to move about freely. However, in one instance where travel was required to distribute Bibles, God provided national Christian people whose job it was to travel the country. Ironically, some were even working for the atheistic government. They were able to conveniently drop off Bibles to Christians around the country without raising any suspicions.

Some people seem to have no problem at all in hearing and receiving guidance from God. For them God seems to open doors almost at will. Regrettably, that is not the same for all of us. Some of us need to seek it more consciously and conscientiously. The confirmation of guidance often comes through Scripture, through other people, or through circumstances. It is interesting to note, however, that God rarely gives major guidance through other people. Usually, He will give it directly to you, and confirm it by others.

This is readily supported through various scriptural passages like Proverbs 12:15, 15:22, and 20:18 which encourage the believer to seek wisdom, counsel, and advice from others in the faith.

If God's will for us is perfect and pleasing, should not His guidance work out accordingly? Yet Paul, writing in Romans, says, "Do not conform any longer to the pattern of this world, but be transformed by the renewing of your mind. Then you will be able to test and approve what God's will is - his good, pleasing and perfect will" (Romans 12:2).

"Test and approve" infers that once we sense what the will of God is for our situation, then we should test and approve that it truly is His will. How can we do that? We refer back to the principles of Scripture and seek confirmation through the indwelling Holy Spirit.

Real guidance from God brings about peace. God will never provide guidance which is contrary to Scriptural principles or which interferes with our relationship with Him. However, it will sometimes bring us into conflict with man-made authority or even go against what might be considered normal expected behavior. God will, at times, bring us to the point where we have to make the decision to follow the crowd, or act upon the knowledge and direction He has given. Others will not always agree with us to confirm the correctness of the path God may have laid out for us. Not even within our church. This is where we need the absolute assurance that we have heard from God. If we have, then all will be well. If not, then any other path we might follow will present us with problems and obstacles.

Even Jesus Needed Guidance

In Luke 4:1 we read that Jesus was led by the Spirit into the desert. If Jesus needed guidance, how much more do we need the Holy Spirit's guidance? Scripture does not always indicate the precise manner in which guidance was given. It is interesting to note that the Holy Spirit kept Paul from preaching in the province of Asia (Acts 16:6). Then we see that when Paul and his companions tried to enter Bithynia, the Holy Spirit would not allow them to do so. How exactly He did this we are not told. We can only conjecture that it might have been through a vision or a dream, as happened on other occasions with Paul and with Peter; or quite literally the Holy Spirit simply closed the door on them.

Even today, as Christians seek guidance in moving forward on a project, or launching out into an unknown area of service, the Spirit of God will close the door and open another at the same time. Paul was not alone in receiving specific and direct guidance from God. We read in biographies of people like John Bunyan, Hudson Taylor, William Carey, and C.T. Studd how they all stepped out in faith and launched into ministries, at home and overseas, when there was no physical or financial support; in fact, just the opposite. They received no encouragement from others, but refused to be dissuaded. They did so because they had received unmistakable guidance from God.

There are many people in Scripture who received very specific guidance from God. From Abraham in the Old Testament all the way to Paul in the New Testament, people were specifically given direction upon their lives regarding tasks to which they were especially called. God chose them for particular tasks for which He specially prepared and equipped them. Joseph received instructions through a dream to take Mary and Jesus and flee to Egypt. He received the return instructions the same way. Paul received guidance by visions. On one occasion, Paul saw a man from Macedonia standing and begging him, "Come over and help us." He left immediately, as he concluded that God was calling him to preach the Gospel in Macedonia (Acts16:10).

Does God speak audibly? There are times we wish He would. Some people indicate that they have heard God speak; and we have no right to question that. If He chooses to speak directly and audibly into your situation, that's wonderful and you are privileged. I do not believe we should limit God. I do not believe we should put God in a box and presume that He will only do what we expect of Him. However, it seems that God speaks more through the Scriptures, through other people, and in our circumstances, rather than directly in an audible voice. When my wife was healed of cancer, I could not say that I actually heard a voice saying, "She will not need the extra surgery," but it certainly made a very deep impression upon me at the time, audibly or otherwise.

It is perplexing, however, that when someone like John Bunyan or Charles Spurgeon state that they have heard from God, we readily accept it. We take them at their word and believe them. Yet when we read a lesser known author who says the same thing, there is a tendency to query the authenticity of the account. Are we then saying that only spiritual giants can hear from God? Who are we to question another person's experience of God? There is no spiritual superiority by hearing or not hearing from God. In fact, the experience can be very humbling.

Perhaps the word we should be considering more than "speak" is "communicate." God communicating with His people is essential for instruction, for guidance, and for specific direction in the conducting of God's business, which is the Church. Again, we are reminded that this is the active ministry of the Holy Spirit. To guide us into all truth inevitably requires some form of communication. How can we be taught, or how can we learn, without receiving instruction?

We know that the message of the Gospel is laid out in Scripture, but the actual work of the redemption of man takes place by the intervention of God the Holy Spirit. If the Holy Spirit cannot speak, then how is the work of redemption conducted? In the book of Acts, it certainly appears that the Holy Spirit gave specific directions to Paul as to where he should and should not go. Whether or not it was audible is immaterial. He certainly communicated His instructions. The same happens today as people are convicted of sin, brought to the realization of their need for a Savior, recognize the gift of salvation through Christ's death on the cross, and are brought to faith in Jesus Christ. All is the work of God's Spirit. The Holy Spirit is part of the Godhead. If God the Holy Spirit does not speak today, then how does the work of regeneration take place?

With regard to salvation, God certainly speaks through literature. When the Bosnian military action was at its height, some Christian people were distributing Billy Graham's *Peace with God* in the hope that people involved in the ethnic conflict would see that there was another way. It was their attempt to bring peace into the situation. Even Christians were only allowed to have a copy of the book if they promised to share it with their unchurched friends.

One sixteen year old girl, whose father was killed on the front line fighting for his country, told about cleaning out his backpack, which arrived home with his body. In sorting through the items, she discovered the book *Peace with God* with a bookmark which indicated he had only read half of it.

She said, "I read the book and have found Jesus Christ. I only hope my father also found Christ before he died!"

Communication from God comes differently to different people. Sometimes it definitely comes as an audible voice (Exodus 3:4). Sometimes He gives instructions through dreams (Matthew 2) and visions (Isaiah 6:1; Revelation 1:12-17). God will speak to us through His Word, as we read it and as we meditate upon it. God also communicates with His children through His still small voice which penetrates our thinking–the quiet inner voice. This calls for us to be quiet before Him, something with which we have difficulty today. We live in a society where people find it hard to be silent or enjoy silence. They find it difficult being alone with their thoughts. But to hear the voice of God, we need to occasionally shut out the world and its demands on our attention, even the legitimate things. Even then, it seems that God does not always communicate as clearly as we would wish. How many times have we wished He would write something in the sky or boom down instructions from on high? But that is not the usual experience.

Peter's guidance was given to him directly through visions and through angels. God can use various means by which He guides us. Yet it is not always through a supernatural occurrence because, as we have already indicated, God has given us intelligence which He expects us to use. Often He will inspire us with ideas and tasks for the benefit of the Church and His kingdom. When Paul was referring to his own teaching, he told Timothy that the Lord would give him understanding directly when he states, "Reflect on what I am saying, for the Lord will give you insight into all this" (2 Timothy 2:7). I reiterate, if the Holy Spirit is allowed to operate in our lives, then we shall be influenced in our understanding directly by Him.

What we can be sure about is this: because God cares for us, we can walk with absolute assurance that our pathway is the best for us. He wants us to live for His glory. We can only do that if our walk is within His plan and purpose, and to do so we need to receive His guidance. There are several references in Psalms which indicate that God's guidance is available if we seek it. God says, "I will instruct you and teach you in the way you should go; I will counsel you and watch over you" (Psalm 32:8). It cannot be more plainly stated than that.

The well known passage from Jeremiah 29:11-13 has been a great blessing to many people. This was the Scripture that my wife and I believe God gave us when we were in a time-restricted crisis regarding accommodation. It confirmed for us that we had to move forward with the decision before us; and time proved it was not only the right decision, but one of incredible blessing; both practically and spiritually. The verses state: "For I know the plans I have for you," declares the Lord, "plans to prosper you and not to harm you, plans to give you hope and a future. Then you will call upon me and come and pray to me, and I will listen to you. You will seek me and find me when you seek me with all your heart." It is the execution of those plans with which we are concerned. Proverbs teaches that "In the heart a man plans his course but the Lord determines his steps" (Proverbs 16:9).

Even if we make the plans, God is still there to direct our steps. The only way that we are going to know the mind and will of God in guidance is to seek Him with all our hearts, which means that we put all else aside, and spend time in His presence in order to see clearly the way forward which, for us, will be the way of blessing.

GUIDE FOR GROUP STUDY

Chapter 4: Does God Guide?

Bible reading: Psalm 32:8-11

8 I will instruct you and teach you in the way you should go;
I will counsel you with my loving eye on you.
9 Do not be like the horse or the mule,
which have no understanding
but must be controlled by bit and bridle
or they will not come to you.
10 Many are the woes of the wicked,
but the Lord's unfailing love
surrounds the one who trusts in him.
11 Rejoice in the Lord and be glad, you righteous;
sing, all you who are upright in heart!

Questions for discussion:

1) Have you ever had a sense that God was guiding you? If so, how did that guidance take place?

2) How were you sure that the guidance came from God?

3) Why would God guide us (His people) and not leave us to our own devices?

4) Should we expect God to guide in every situation, including everyday activity?

5) In Judges 6, beginning with verse 36, Gideon laid out a fleece to test what he thought he heard God promise. Do you think it is right to put out a "fleece," as Gideon did, in seeking to know God's guidance? (Read Judges 6:36-40 if need be)

6) Specifically, how should someone seek the guidance of God?

CHAPTER FIVE:
Does God Provide?

"And my God will meet all your needs according to his glorious riches in Christ Jesus."

Philippians 4:19

In September 1957, I returned to Bible College for my second year. I had arrived without sufficient funds to cover the fees for the year. This was not unusual, as most students found it difficult to come up with adequate resources to cover all costs and other eventualities at the beginning of a school year. Previously, we had been allowed to hand in our fees throughout the school year as funds became available. That year the rules had changed, but we were unaware of the change until we arrived back at college. The new rule was that all fees had to be paid by noon on the first Saturday after school commenced. It appeared that students had been professing to "live by faith," but the faith was not producing much living!

I had five days to bring in the balance–which was not insignificant. I prayed about it nonchalantly throughout the week, thinking that God would answer prayer and that funds would come in through the mail. As letters arrived for me, I eagerly opened them, only to find most were wishing me blessings as I commenced a new term, but none of them held any monetary gifts.

Friday arrived and I fully expected that this was the day that God would provide, but even Friday brought nothing. I was in England, where mail is delivered on Saturdays. In my mind, I was confident that the Saturday mail would bring in the funds. The mail arrived with a letter for me, but no funds. I knew that mail sometimes went to the college instead of to the student residence, so I immediately went off to the college expecting to see a letter there–no letter! By now it was 10:30 a.m. and I had until noon to come up with the funds.

I returned to my bedroom at the student residence and got down on my knees to pray. While praying, I asked God to give me some passage of Scripture that might bring me some reassurance that I would see my prayer answered. The verse of Scripture which came to me provided all the assurance I needed. It was, "Be still and know that I am God" (Psalm 46:10). I felt strongly it was just for me in my situation. I felt confident that somehow, someway, God would provide the necessary funds before noon.

I left the room and went to have morning coffee with some other students. I returned to my room at 11:30 a.m. There on my bed was an envelope which had arrived by registered mail. The late delivery was because someone had to sign for it. It was an incredible moment to see the envelope, but what was even more amazing, was the letter inside the envelope. It came from a lady whom I did not know. It came from a place in England to which I had never visited. What's more, the letter said, "I understand you are in need of funds for your schooling. Here is some money. It will cover your fees and the extra funds can go towards your textbooks!" Needless to say, I was blown away. I felt my faith had been rewarded and my prayer answered.

Although the provision of those funds was a miracle to me, about six months later I learned how the miracle had happened. It was very simple, and one might say it was no miracle at all. One of my peers had been instructed by a lady that if, after he returned to college, he came across a student in financial need he was to let her know. While discussing the new rule regarding tuition payments with fellow students, I had unwittingly indicated that I was looking for God to do something for me during that week and, of course, He did, through this lady. Whether you want to call this coincidence or anything else, the way it happened to me was that God provided for my needs at the right moment. It certainly strengthened my faith and enabled me to further trust God to supply my needs later in life.

As Bible College students, we were often called upon to go out and lead Sunday services, especially in small churches where there were no pastors or churches that were waiting for the arrival of a new pastor. Most of these churches would provide a small honorarium for the speaking engagement. However, not all did so. Some church leaders thought that because we were students they were doing us a favor by allowing us to speak. They considered it "practice" for our later ministry. One Sunday evening, I went by bus to just such a church, obviously not knowing their thinking on this issue.

I had just enough money for the bus fare to the church but not enough for the ride back to college. I had assumed that the church would make a small gift of cash, thus providing the fare for the return trip. I was wrong. After arriving, I was informed that it was not their practice to provide students with an honorarium. Throughout the service, I was wondering how God would provide–or would I be taking a very long walk, about 15 miles, back to school?

Rightly or wrongly, I then assumed that a gift would come through someone in the congregation. As the people filed out after the service, I stood at the door shaking hands. As I looked around I saw that the number of people left in the church was getting decidedly smaller by the minute. Finally, we were down to the last person and the janitor, who was waiting to lock up. The very last gentleman shook my hand and in the centre of his hand was a note which he transferred to mine. He simply said, "God bless you" and went out the door. I looked in my hand to see the note. It could well have been a note to say what he thought of the sermon from this budding preacher. It was in fact, a ten shilling note–enough bus fare to get me back several times over. I often wondered why God left it to the very last person. It certainly was a faith tester and a faith builder.

How many times have we listened to a request for financial help from a missionary or received an appeal through the mail to support an orphan or other worthy causes? Many of them presented a great need, were worthwhile causes, and tugged at our heart strings creating a desire to give. There are times we must respond because we may be the channel to provide for the need. There is a danger however, that our heart can sometimes overrule our pocket book. It's fine to think that God will provide if you make the commitment, but God expects us to act responsibly in making such a decision. If we think that God will always come through with promised funds then we could say "yes" to every appeal we receive, and to every missionary who needs support for his or her work. I don't believe that this is right or prudent. God has given us intelligence which we must use to guide the heart and the purse strings. As much as our heart would motivate us to help, it must always be supported by our ability to keep the commitment. Making a pledge before God is a serious thing and should never be taken lightly. However, from experience I do believe that God provides for us when we seriously make a pledge and attempt to fulfill the commitment.

I am sure you have experienced the stark reality of life when your bank statement shows zero balance. My wife and I faced just such a situation some years ago. At the time I was working in a commission-only job. Everything was going along fine until the sales began to disappear and the commission checks became smaller and smaller until they became non-existent. We literally had nothing in the bank. We were forced to sit down and discuss what we could do and how to proceed.

We spent time in prayer together and then separately. It was not long before my wife came down from praying in the bedroom and simply asked, "Did you send off that money for our pledge to... ?" She mentioned the name of the missionary. I admitted that I had not because of our declining bank balance.

She replied, "I think that is our problem. We made a commitment and we have broken it. I think you should send the money."

There was no money in the bank and I was very reluctant to draw a check. I had never had one bounce before, and I did not want to see that happen now. However, because the funds were to be sent overseas, I wrote the check and sent it off. Within a few days of making the commitment, sales began again and before the check came back to the bank, there were adequate funds to cover it. Keeping a pledge made before God is extremely important.

In recent years, my work allowed me to visit many countries in the former communist bloc, from Russia in the north to Albania in the south. During those visits there, I witnessed and learned of God's provision for a people under oppression; a people who had suffered much persecution under the communist regimes. After the collapse of communism, many stories came to light which would cheer and encourage the hearts of all Christians. God's miraculous provision was what the Church needed at that time and that was exactly what God provided. The Church in the West might question modern day miracles and put God in a box, but that just limits spiritual vision, thinking, and expectations.

God Provides as We Trust

In the city of Budapest, Hungary during the harsh communist days, the Church generally met with much trepidation. The times of meetings could not be publicized, and were only known to the Christians. This helped prevent, but did not eradicate, the presence of informers who would turn up at the meetings and promptly inform the authorities as to who was at the meeting, and what took place.

Every month on a particular weekend, a Christian conference was held at the Free Christian Church. This conference offered teaching and general encouragement for any believer in Eastern Europe, provided he or she could get to Budapest. Although the dates were never published, the church was always full. People would come from many places, including neighboring countries. One weekend, fifty people came down from East Germany for the conference. These people were generally poor and could not afford hotels. Even if they could, hotels were places for the Christians to avoid because the rooms were bugged and strict registration (including copying your passport) was standard procedure. Knowing this, the local Christians took it upon themselves to open up their homes to accommodate the visitors. Generally, the local Christians had very small homes or apartments. Most visitors expected to sleep on the floor.

At the end of the Saturday meeting, the pastor's wife would ask who needed accommodation, and would link people together with those who were opening up their homes to the visitors. When relating the story to me, the pastor's wife said that on one particular weekend, after every home had maximized the number of people they could accommodate, there were still eighteen people left with nowhere to stay. She told me that it was the responsibility of the pastor and his wife to accommodate those with nowhere to go. Their apartment in Budapest was probably no more than 500 square feet and consisted of three rooms plus a small kitchen and a bathroom. Already living there was the pastor, his wife, their teenage son, and another elderly lady who permanently resided with them.

The pastor's wife ran home to inform her boarder, "We have eighteen people coming to stay overnight."

Elizabeth, the boarder, did not ask where they would sleep. Instead she said, "What are we going to give them to eat?" In Budapest at that time of night, you could not go out and find a supermarket to purchase food. All stores closed at noon on Saturday and did not reopen until Monday morning.

The pastor's wife indicated that she had expected visitors and had prepared accordingly. She said that she had purchased a chicken for the occasion.

Elizabeth's reply was, "Have you seen the size of the chicken?"

"Yes," said the pastor's wife. "It is three pounds!" She then said, "We will pray over the chicken, cook the chicken, and then serve it up."

And that is exactly what they did. The chicken was prayed over, cooked, served up, and twenty-two people ate from a three pound chicken and there was chicken left over! When I came home and shared the story with my family, the first response from my daughter was, "That's the same as Jesus feeding the five thousand people!" Did God provide for them, or was it mere coincidence that you could continually carve enough meat from a three pound chicken to feed twenty-two people?

However, the sequel to this story is even more fascinating. Being somewhat awed by this account, we were reiterating the event to another pastor in another East European country. He seemed to be less than impressed by what we were telling him. Emphasizing the miraculous, we said, "Twenty-two people ate from a three pound chicken. Don't you think that was a miracle?"

His reply stunned us. "Yes, brother, yes brother," he replied in a nonchalant manner. "We think so every time it happens to us!"

We found ourselves trying to impress a man who was so God-oriented, that for him *not* to expect God to intervene, and take care of situations, would have been unnatural. For him, miracles were not extraordinary–but simply God taking care of His people.

I asked the pastor's wife in Budapest this question: "Why is it that you see miracles here in Eastern Europe and we rarely do in the West?"

Her response was immediate, but quite natural and humble. She replied, "I don't know why you don't see them. We just do as much as we can and we leave the rest to God!" What a simple, yet profound, answer. They simply expect God to pick up where they leave off, and He does.

Can you imagine having to worship in a rented hall for over forty years? This was the experience of the same Free Christian Church in Budapest. Since the Second World War, the congregation met in various places for worship, renting larger and larger premises as their church grew in numbers.

Then, in March 1985, a member mentioned to the pastor that a derelict restaurant was for sale in the city and suggested he should look at it, with the idea of turning it into a church. He did just that and met with the lady owner, who happened to be Roman Catholic. She was asking 4,000,000 forints for the building, which at the time, was the equivalent to approximately $120,000. Upon hearing that the intention was to turn the place into a church, the owner immediately reduced the price to 3,000,000 forints, or $90,000.

Receiving a positive response from the congregation, the pastor signed an offer agreeing to purchase the building and guaranteeing that the total purchase price would be paid by the end of June. This was in March. Because the church had been trying to save for their own building in the future, they actually already had ten percent of the purchase price in the bank. All they had to do was raise the other 90% in three months!

It is an understatement to say that these 200 people gave sacrificially. The average weekly wage was about $30, and therefore it took very little to make their giving sacrificial. Some people had been saving for five years for new furniture, new appliances or even a family holiday. They abandoned their plans and gave the money to the building fund. Pensioners who had no savings brought family heirlooms or jewellery with sentimental value, to be sold on behalf of the new church. The members extended themselves to their financial limits and beyond, but it was not enough. By the first week of June, the church had collected half of the money needed, about 1,500,000 forints or $45,000. There was exactly one month left to raise the other half. The church was called to prayer. They asked the Lord what else could be done. They had given everything they possibly could.

Within two weeks, the pastor received a letter asking him to go with some elders of the church to the local branch of the Hungarian National Bank. Upon arrival at the bank, they were told that a deposit was about to be made into the church's account from an estate of a deceased West German lady, who had died three years previously. The lady had visited the church in the past and was very impressed and interested in their work. The estate had just been settled and the church was to receive an inheritance. When the pastor enquired as to how much the inheritance was, the bank official said, "One and a half million forints!"($45,000) It was exactly the amount they needed to purchase the derelict restaurant. They had all the money in place with two weeks to spare. Was that just a remarkable coincidence? I am reminded of Jesus' words, "...your father knows what you need before you ask him" (Matthew 6:8).

A number of years ago in a small Polish village not far from the Slovakian border, a very courageous doctor began an annual week-long evangelistic tent meeting. It was courageous because the communists were still very much in power, and he was under constant observation by the authorities. It would appear, however, that he made the right judgment call because people were eager to hear the Gospel. Every year, over 4,000 people would flock to this small village for the meetings. The event was nothing short of a miracle, considering it was happening within a communist regime. Buses had to be hired to convey the many people wanting to travel from distant places. There was nothing like it throughout Eastern Europe. It seemed that God had a sense of humor–buses belonging to the atheistic communist regime were used to bring people to hear the Gospel.

I, along with a colleague, had the privilege of traveling to this village to experience for ourselves the week's activity. At that time Bibles were scarce, but we were able to surreptitiously transport a van-load of Bibles to that place. These were hurriedly unloaded, before prying eyes could see and inform the authorities. The people we met during that week showed nothing but excitement at experiencing the blessing of meeting together to hear the preaching of God's Word. It highlighted for me just how privileged we are in the West to openly hear preaching in our pulpits Sunday by Sunday without fear of reprisal.

Several years later, four of us visited the doctor while he was planning the event. He was particularly concerned because he had no funds to hire the buses. Few people owned cars, so the buses were necessary; but he was seriously considering whether or not he could financially proceed with the program. We, as a group, were on a four-country tour to see various projects. We carried some reserve cash with us ready to donate to any worthy project or situation which we considered needed assistance. We recognized this as one such situation. We mentioned that we only had $1,200 which we could contribute towards helping him rent the buses. Tears immediately filled his eyes. "That is the exact amount needed to hire the buses!" was his tearful response. How did we know? We didn't, but God knew. The event went ahead as planned.

Faith's Reward

When we think of God's provision we might think of that great man of faith, George Müller. He moved from Germany, his place of birth, to England in 1829. It was there that he was so moved by the plight of thousands of orphaned or abandoned children that his heart drove him to provide for them. While carrying out his overwhelming task he said, "Now, if I, a poor man, simply by prayer and faith, obtained without asking any individual, the means for establishing and carrying on an orphan-house; there would be something which, with the Lord's blessing, might be instrumental in strengthening the faith of the children of God, besides being a testimony to the consciences of the unconverted of the reality of the things of God."[1]

Supported by that element of trust in God, George Müller opened his first orphanage in Bristol, England in 1836. It housed thirty children. It was a tremendous leap of faith and a huge challenge. Yet this was to be just the beginning of many more homes for children and his life's work, which was sealed with the approval of God. He eventually cared for approximately ten thousand children. That was a monumental task when all the provisions had to be provided by faith. Without issuing any appeals for funds, Müller had over three million dollars donated over his 63 years of ministry to orphaned children, which was a huge sum during the nineteenth century.

Five years after opening his first home he wrote, "This way of living brings the Lord remarkably near. He is, as it were, morning by morning inspecting our stores, that accordingly He may send help. Greater and more manifest nearness of the Lord's presence I have never had, than when after breakfast there were no means for dinner, and then the Lord provided the dinner for more than one hundred persons; or when, after dinner, there were no means for tea, and yet the Lord provided the tea; and all without one human being having been informed about our need."[2] Such was the constant provision of God.

One of the greatest impressions left upon me over my years of travel in Eastern Europe was from the words of a lady I met in Serbia. Her husband had just returned from spending a year in a prisoner of war camp in Bosnia. He considered his release a miracle, and was overjoyed to be home with his family. Together, with their two children, they lived in pitiful conditions; they had one room and a kitchen. Without any prompting, the wife said, "I have come to learn that material possessions are worthless. To have spiritual peace means everything!" To make such a statement when you have money in the bank is far less meaningful than when you possess very little of this world's goods. That family had nothing!

I am reminded that Paul wrote to the church in Philippi, "And my God will meet all your needs according to his glorious riches in Christ Jesus" (Philippians 4:19). Some people seem to have changed the word *needs* to *wants*, but that is not what the Scripture states.

The Psalmist says, "I was young and now I am old, yet I have never seen the righteous forsaken or their children begging bread. They are always generous and lend freely; their children will be blessed" (Psalm 37:25-26). Such is God's care for His children. We can never out-give God. If we care for others and share what we have, then the Lord provides accordingly (Proverbs 19:17). Our obedience of Scripture will bring its just reward as we read, "Honour the Lord with your wealth, with the first-fruits of all your crops; then your barns will be filled to overflowing, and your vats will brim over with new wine" (Proverbs 3:9-10).

While God provides for our needs, He does expect us to be responsible. In other words, if we expect God to provide, we need to be good stewards of that which He has entrusted to us. Why should He put bread on the table if we squander what He has already given us?

When we consider God providing for us, we mostly

think in terms of financial provision, but God provides for His children in a myriad of ways throughout life. God's provision covers both physical and spiritual needs. The needs of our spiritual life and Christian walk are given through God's Word and the ministry of the Holy Spirit. He also provides our daily physical needs such as food, clothes, and shelter. We are often unaware of the provision He has made for us. However, the Scripture is explicit in laying out the priority when it states, "seek first his kingdom and his righteousness, and all these things will be given to you as well. Therefore do not worry about tomorrow..." (Matthew 6:33). In other words, Jesus is saying, "Do not worry, God will provide." What better consolation can we have than the very words of the Lord Jesus Christ?

GUIDE FOR GROUP STUDY

Chapter 5: Does God Provide?

Bible reading: Matthew 6:25-34

25 "Therefore I tell you, do not worry about your life, what you will eat or drink; or about your body, what you will wear. Is not life more than food, and the body more than clothes? 26 Look at the birds of the air; they do not sow or reap or store away in barns, and yet your heavenly Father feeds them. Are you not much more valuable than they? 27 Can any one of you by worrying add a single hour to your life?

28 "And why do you worry about clothes? See how the flowers of the field grow. They do not labor or spin. 29 Yet I tell you that not even Solomon in all his splendor was dressed like one of these. 30 If that is how God clothes the grass of the field, which is here today and tomorrow is thrown into the fire, will he not much more clothe you—you of little faith? 31 So do not worry, saying, 'What shall we eat?' or 'What shall we drink?' or 'What shall we wear?' 32 For the pagans run after all these things, and your heavenly Father knows that you need them. 33 But seek first his kingdom and his righteousness, and all these things will be given to you as well. 34 Therefore do not worry about tomorrow, for tomorrow will worry about itself. Each day has enough trouble of its own.

Questions for discussion:

1) Do you believe God provides for His children today? If so, in what way(s) does He do this?

2) In our day of plenty, what do we need God to provide?

3) What does God show us by providing what we need?

4) How do your "needs and wants" affect your requests for God's provision?

5) If your motive is right and your purpose is honorable, such as wanting to build a church, would God always provide the funds? Why or why not?

6) Tell of an instance where you know God has provided, either for you or for someone else.

CHAPTER SIX:
DOES GOD PROTECT?

"I will say of the Lord, he is my refuge and my fortress, my God, in whom I trust."

Psalm 91:2

Our journey began in Debrecen, on the east side of Hungary and ended in Tirana, the capital of Albania. It was a fifty-seven hour drive, during which time we had seven hours of sleep and one main meal. This was a trip in 1991 to deliver six ambulances, which Eurovangelism was donating to the Albanian Ministry of Health. I had the privilege of being one of the ambulance drivers in the convoy of ambulances and mini-buses. The ambulances had been refurbished and, together with the other vehicles, were loaded to the hilt with medical supplies, other humanitarian aid, and 11,000 copies of the first Bible in the Albanian language.

We left Debrecen early on a Tuesday morning and arrived in Tirana Thursday evening. If ever there was a journey which required the protection of God, it was this one. At that time, the Bosnian war was in progress and our route took us within twelve miles of the fighting. We had to carry drums of gas for all the vehicles because none was available in what was the former Yugoslavia. All fuel was being used in the military conflict. Also, at any time, any of our ambulances or vehicles could have been commandeered by the military for their own use.

The Yugoslav border guards were less than cooperative and forced us to unload every vehicle in the convoy; which included six ambulances plus three other vehicles pulling trailers. The guards were concerned about the Bibles as at that time, two million Albanians lived within the Yugoslav borders. The guards were not convinced that we would take all the Bibles on into Albania. They only allowed us to take what we could fit into two trailers. These were then custom-sealed to ensure we took them out of the country. The rest of the Bibles were placed in storage at the border at our cost, to be retrieved at a later date by the national Hungarian Christians on the team. From 7:30 p.m. until 3:30 a.m. we unloaded and reloaded the vehicles. Within one hour of leaving the border, we stopped to rest but were quickly surrounded by police who confiscated our cameras because we were in a war zone.

After a two hour rest, we continued our journey south. I do not believe it was coincidental that at the time we were closest to the fighting, which was very early in the morning, the clouds opened up and we traveled through a torrential rain storm. The storm continued for an hour or so while we drove many miles. The weather cleared once we were out of the military conflict area. We drove all that day until 11:30 p.m.

While a few of us had the privilege of sleeping at a small hotel, some of the group had to stay on guard duty throughout the night. Because of the local poverty and scarcity of goods, our vehicles were an easy target for predatory gangs.

When we finally reached Albania, we were astonished to discover how primitive and poverty stricken the country was. Children were dressed in little more than rags, and had no shoes. We were warned that they would steal anything because this was their way of life. Most of the roads were either made of gravel or in desperate need of repair. Geographically the country is beautiful, with mountains and valleys and a coastline along the Adriatic Sea. It is seventy-five percent mountainous which we found quite treacherous in driving from the border to the capital, Tirana. That trip took about eight hours, as the roads over the mountains were narrow with many hairpin bends. The sides of the roads fell away many hundreds of feet down to the valleys below.

We drove the last forty kilometres in pitch darkness. Our convoy would suddenly come upon people walking, people on bicycles, animals, and occasionally trucks, tractors or other vehicles, all without lights. It was apparent that very few vehicles in the country were in good running order. Most vehicles were more than forty years old. In spite of these potential hazards, it was a miracle that we were not involved in any accidents and did not careen over the edge to the valley below. Our convoy arrived without incident. Many people were praying for the trip, and all team members agreed that they had never felt more prayer covering and protection than they did on that trip.

God's protection is sometimes difficult to recognize, mostly because we are unaware that we have received it. Unless there is some identifiable divine intervention in a specific event, how is one to know that protection, resulting in safety, has been provided? As with many of God's blessings, it is not until after the event that we see God's hand in it. On my travels to Poland I learned the following story.

At the age of eighteen, a young Polish man came to admit that his life was in a mess. He had made mistakes and felt lonely and abandoned. It was true that life had not been very kind to him. He was an orphan and had been in foster care most of his life. One couple had attempted to care for him and had sought to instruct him in the Roman Catholic traditions. Consequently, he turned to the local priest for help. He poured out his heart as to where he had gone wrong and sought help in restoration. He needed sympathetic counsel and good spiritual advice at that moment.

Unfortunately, the priest was anything but helpful. In fact, his attitude only deepened the despair in this young man's life. He was sent away with the words, "God will never forgive you because you did not recite the preconfessional liturgy," ringing in his ears. He vowed at that point never to enter a church again.

Eventually he married and became the father of three children. However, at the age of twenty-eight, his life was still plagued with problems. His marriage had not been a success. He and his wife lived separate lives under the same roof. He agreed with his wife that a divorce was the answer to their situation. While he waited for the arrangements to become finalized, he became extremely depressed.

Early one February morning, he decided that he had nothing more to offer this world. He made the decision to end it that day. So with the temperature outside well below zero, he made his way to a main highway. He walked to the middle of the road where he laid down and waited for a truck to run over him. Two hours later, with frost forming on him as he lay in the road, he was still waiting for the first vehicle to come along. He could not understand it. Normally this was a busy road. Bewildered, cold, and totally disillusioned, he got up and went home. His wife was not there. When she came home, he never mentioned his attempted suicide.

The next day, his wife revealed where she had been when he had arrived home. She explained that she had spent time with some friends who had invited her to a home Bible study. She suggested that he, too, join them at the next meeting. This he agreed to do and it was at that meeting that both he and his wife made decisions to receive Jesus Christ as their Lord and Savior. Needless to say, their lives were completely turned around. Three weeks later, their divorce papers were torn up, their family was wonderfully united, and their love for each other was new and fresh; the same as their love for the Savior they had just found. It could have been a totally different story with a tragic ending. Instead, a miracle of protection in the life of this young man made all the difference.

Miraculous Protection

In the chapter *Does God Provide?* I wrote about how

God provided the funds for the Free Christian Church in Budapest, Hungary to purchase a derelict restaurant to renovate into a church. It took some time to get the place in order for regular congregational worship. Because of their lack of funds, most of the work was carried out by members of the congregation. Thus every week, the place was busy with volunteers doing whatever was asked of them to assist in the building process. People came after work, and especially on Saturdays, offering their help.

It became the custom of the church leaders to organize a regular Friday evening prayer session, particularly to pray about the renovations and the future of the church. It was during one of those prayer meetings that an unusual suggestion was made. One of the deacons stated that he felt the group should be praying about the roof. When asked, "What about the roof?" he really had no answer. He said, "I don't know why, but I feel impressed that we should be praying about the roof."

The pastor knew from experience that if this impression was coming from God, then they dare not ignore it. So they prayed about the roof. It was not long before the answer came as to why they prayed.

One Saturday morning, there were about forty people working in the building. One person was working in the rafters of the old restaurant roof. In his attempt to remove some of the old wood, his hammer accidentally caught something metallic and dislodged it from the rafters. Suddenly there was a huge bang and a metallic clang as the object fell from the roof to the concrete floor below. Fortunately, it caused no injuries when falling, but what was even more incredible was that the object turned out to be an unexploded World War II bomb, which had been lodged in the roof for forty years. It was a miracle of protection.

The police were called who, in turn, called the army. The bomb squad arrived. They confirmed that the bomb was indeed still live, and could not understand why it had not exploded when it hit the ground. If it had, probably the forty people there would have been killed and the place blown apart. The officer in charge of the bomb squad said to the pastor, "You are very lucky people. This could have killed you all."

The pastor's response was, "We are not lucky people; we have a great God. He had already warned us to pray about the roof of this building. We did not know why at the time, but now we do."

One of the hardest things to understand is: if God is our Protector, why do Christians have to suffer? It appears to us that when we suffer, God is not protecting. If God is sovereign and in control, why does it seem as if He does not intervene and stop the persecution or suffering? One aspect, of course, is that if our road was always smooth, we would never know when it was that God carried us over the bumps.

Late one night, a policeman knocked on the door of a pastor's house in a small Romanian village. If you have ever had a policeman arrive on your doorstep, you will know that initially it brings trepidation before you learn why he is there. For pastors in Eastern Europe, it usually meant only one thing; they were being arrested or at least being taken in for questioning regarding Christian activities. With some concern, the pastor went to the door and was very disturbed to be confronted with a police officer. He quickly recognized the policeman as one who was an avowed enemy of the church. Before the pastor could say anything, the policeman spoke. "Don't be afraid," said the officer, "there is something I want to talk to you about."

The pastor invited him in, not knowing what to expect. They sat down and the officer started the conversation by asking, "Pastor, you had a meeting last night in the wooden house up on the hill, didn't you?"

"Yes," said the pastor, nodding assent.

"And you sang a number of songs, didn't you?"

Again the pastor nodded, "Yes, we did, but why do you ask?"

"It's this that I want to talk with you about," the policemen went on. "We had been informed that you were going to have a meeting last night in the wooden house, so we made plans to arrest you, but something hindered us from doing so. Two other men and I watched the house from our hiding place and saw all you believers walking up the hill and going into the wooden house one by one. You started your meeting and we decided to let you continue for a while, to be sure to arrest everyone involved. When you started singing, we thought it was time to move in on you. But as we were walking up the hill towards the house, instead of the singing getting louder and clearer, it gradually seemed to fade away into the distance!

"When we arrived at the house we stopped at the door, and listened by the windows. The house was completely silent! The place seemed to be totally deserted. As we stood on top of the hill outside the house in the silence of the evening, we began to hear the singing again but coming from down the hill somewhere. We concluded that you had all managed to slip out of the back door of the house unnoticed, and got together in another place.

"Quickly we went down the hill trying to locate where you were. The singing seemed to be getting closer the further we went down the hill and the nearer we got to the bridge. When we reached the bridge, the singing faded again and sounded as though it was coming from some distance away. We stood there at the bridge for some time. We heard you sing many songs, but could not decide where it was coming from.

"After a while, we agreed that the sound must be coming from the wooden house up the hill after all, so we began making our way up the hill. The nearer we got to the house, the louder the singing became, so we were assured that's where you were. But then the strange phenomenon happened all over again. As we approached the house for the second time, the singing seemed to elude us and we found the house as silent as before.

"By this time, we were utterly bewildered and did not know what to think. We decided to search through the village, up and down until we found you. As we walked, we could hear the singing. Sometimes it seemed close, and other times much further away, virtually coming from all directions. We were totally unsuccessful in finding you, and finally, at midnight, we gave up and decided to go back to the police station. To our complete and utter amazement, on our way back we saw you Christians coming down from the wooden house on the hill, going back to your homes. We were absolutely speechless!

"Whatever happened last night, I cannot explain... but I felt the power of God protecting you and I was afraid. In fact, I was so afraid that I trembled, and made a deal with God. I said, "Grant me to see tomorrow and I shall turn my life over to you... and that is what I want to talk to you about, Pastor."

The pastor, who had been listening attentively to the policeman's story, was overwhelmed by what God had done the night before, and overjoyed to find that out of this experience, the officer now wanted to commit his life to Christ and join the persecuted. When a non-believer can feel and recognize the protection of God for His children, then you know it is real. The pastor and the people, who were intent on their time of worship, had no idea that God was protecting them as they worshipped.

Psalm 40 is often used to comfort and strengthen the Christian in times of trial. It illustrates the reward for waiting upon God, and waiting for God. It shows the resultant blessing of being lifted up out of the mire, out of a slimy pit and having our feet set solidly on a rock with a song of praise on our lips. David makes it clear that, "Blessed is the man who makes the Lord his trust" (Psalm 40:2-4). How many times do we find ourselves needing to be reminded of this spiritual principle? David suffered much at the hands of his enemies and experienced God's hand of intervention while going through it, yet he still needed to declare, "Do not withhold your mercy from me, O Lord; may your love and your truth always protect me" (Psalm 40:11).

Border crossings in Eastern Europe were always unpredictable. Sometimes it was pleasant, other times it was formidable. It seemed that the communists were paranoid regarding the importation of Bibles. For instance, at one time, everyone going into Russia was asked if they had Bibles in their possession, regardless of who they were; such was the communists' fear of God's Word entering their country. They considered that Bibles would corrupt their people. It was often at the border crossings where God blinded the eyes of the guards searching suitcases for Bibles or other Christian literature, even when the books or Bibles came into view. From the detailed searching of suitcases, pockets, and wallets, it was incredible how the eyes of the guards were blinded to books, papers, and documents being carried across the borders. It seemed that the literature was made invisible. With God, all things are possible. Jeremiah the prophet declared this confidence in God when he stated, "Ah Sovereign Lord, you have made the heavens and the earth by your great power and outstretched arm. Nothing is too hard for you" (Jeremiah 32:17).

God's Undeniable Protection

It is hard to imagine that the largest Baptist church in Europe is in the former communist country of Romania. It is Emmanuel Baptist Church in the town of Oradea. I had the privilege of being at the opening of that impressive church, erected soon after the collapse of communism. Although built to accommodate 2,300 people, when we arrived at 7:45 a.m., we found the new building already filled to capacity and overflowing. The service was due to commence at 8:00 a.m. Every available space was filled. The aisles were filled with people standing, the balcony was jammed, the foyer was filled, the overflow rooms were full, and people stood outside the church in the rain. An estimated 7,000 people were at that first meeting, which lasted almost five hours!

It was during the three hour evening service that an unscheduled event took place. While the choir was singing, a man came running in and jumped onto the platform brandishing a large machete-type knife. Attempts by ushers to disarm him were met with threats. The five or six pastors on the platform stood and surrounded the man.

Pastor Nick Gheorghita's enquiry, "What is it you want?" was met with, "I'm possessed by Satan and am here to kill you all!"

Pastor Gheorghita placed his hand on the man's shoulder and quietly said, "You don't want to kill us. We love you. Why don't we pray for you, but first put that knife down on the pulpit."

The man obeyed and was led off the platform by Pastor Gheorghita, who placed his arm around the man.

Dr. Paul Negrut, the senior pastor, asked the congregation to stand as he led in a prayer for the man. It was a dynamic prayer. The atmosphere was electric. Dr. Negrut reminded the people that the Church is never far away from the reality of spiritual warfare. The services closed that day with many people responding to the Gospel. The day could have ended very differently. Yet it ended as a testimony to the grace and protection of God for His people.

One of the greatest promises of deliverance and protection is found in Psalm 91. Under the inspiration of the Holy Spirit, the psalmist wrote these words, "Because he loves me," says the Lord, "I will rescue him, I will protect him, for he acknowledges my name. He will call upon me, and I will answer him; I will be with him in trouble, I will deliver him and honour him. With long life will I satisfy him and show him my salvation" (Psalm 91:14-16).

When we find ourselves in a situation where we are desperately looking for God's protection, or needing His deliverance, our first line of defense and support will come directly from the Word of God. It has been given to us for our encouragement, for our exhortation, and to provide us strength in times of need. We can know and be assured that the arm of the Lord is more powerful than any obstacle or opposition that might arise. God is not challenged by any situation which calls for His intervention. As David says, our part is to learn to trust Him and then exercise that trust. God will do the rest.

In the wonderful prayer of Jesus in John 17, He prays for the protection of His followers from Satan, the enemy. Jesus, praying to His Father says, "My prayer is not that you take them out of the world but that you protect them from the evil one" (John 17:15). This is obviously the greatest, and most necessary, protection needed by the Christian. Spiritual protection supersedes any physical deliverance for which we might pray.

God's protection often comes through the ministry of angels. This is not as uncommon as we might think. The Scripture supports this when it states, "Are not all angels ministering spirits sent to serve those who will inherit salvation?" (Hebrews 1:14)

God uses men and angels to minister to and protect His children. It has been suggested that many of those people mentioned in Hebrews, on that roll call of those who lived by faith, would have received the comfort and support of ministering angels in their hour of persecution and suffering, yet they still had to endure the pain. Jesus also was strengthened by an angel when praying in the garden of Gethsemane. Other examples abound throughout Scripture. There are numerous creditable stories of earthly visitations of angels. Corrie ten Boom writes about the protection from angels she experienced while in the Nazi Ravensbrück prison camp. Some people have experienced the presence of angels while being trapped in accidents. Others have seen angels near the time of their departure from this life.

We have a friend in England whose car broke down very late at night. The car engine just died while she was traveling along in the country; only empty fields around and no other cars in sight. As the engine sputtered out, she was able to coast into a small paved area made for emergency purposes. Everything around was silent. She bowed her head asking God for help. She looked up to see a car reversing into the same area just ahead of her. A lady jumped out, came to the window and asked if her husband could help. A man got out of the car ahead and asked for the hood to be raised. He put his hand on the battery and suggested our friend start the car. The engine came to life immediately. They promised to follow her home, which was a long way out of the way for anyone travelling on that particular road. But they did just that, and followed her for miles. As our friend drove up to her house, she looked behind to wave goodbye, but the car was nowhere to be seen! Her belief that this was an angelic visit was confirmed all the more when, the next day, her car would not start and in fact, had to be towed in and repaired by a mechanic before it would operate again.

Unquestionably, angels have been sent to comfort and protect; to stand on guard when certain children of God have been in danger. In the psalms, we find this clear statement: "For he will command his angels concerning you to guard you in all your ways" (Psalm 91:11). We may not know it or even be aware of it at the time, but God's protection is never far away. Another psalm assures the Christian of comfort and the assurance that he is never far from the watchful eye of his Father.

We read, "The Lord watches over you–the Lord is your shade at your right hand, the sun will not harm you by day, nor the moon by night. The Lord will keep you from all harm–he will watch over your life; the Lord will watch over your coming and going both now and forevermore" (Psalm 121:5-8).

Sometimes we are recipients of God's blessing from our own actions. David declares, "Blessed is he who has regard for the weak, the Lord delivers him in times of trouble. The Lord will protect him and preserve his life"(Psalm 41:1-2). Although we can never earn it, this Scripture would indicate that we can receive God's blessing of protection and care as we offer compassion to those who are weak or less fortunate.

There will always be times in life when we cannot understand why, in the physical, God did not provide protection. At those times we must defer to God's sovereignty. God's sovereignty must take precedence over our desires and prayers, because God's long term spiritual plans for us will bring greater blessing. We can be assured that because God loves us unconditionally, He holds us in His hands and has our best interests at heart. Whatever He sees fit to bring into our lives will bring Him ultimate glory. We would not wish, or pray, for anything less.

GUIDE FOR GROUP STUDY

Chapter 6: Does God Protect?

Bible reading: Psalm 91

1 Whoever dwells in the shelter of the Most High
    will rest in the shadow of the Almighty.
2 I will say of the Lord, "He is my refuge and my fortress,
    my God, in whom I trust."

3 Surely he will save you
    from the fowler's snare
    and from the deadly pestilence.
4 He will cover you with his feathers,
    and under his wings you will find refuge;
    his faithfulness will be your shield and rampart.
5 You will not fear the terror of night,
    nor the arrow that flies by day,
6 nor the pestilence that stalks in the darkness,
    nor the plague that destroys at midday.
7 A thousand may fall at your side,
    ten thousand at your right hand,
    but it will not come near you.
8 You will only observe with your eyes
    and see the punishment of the wicked.

9 If you say, "The Lord is my refuge,"
    and you make the Most High your dwelling,
10 no harm will overtake you,
    no disaster will come near your tent.
11 For he will command his angels concerning you

to guard you in all your ways;
12 they will lift you up in their hands,
  so that you will not strike your foot against a stone.
13 You will tread on the lion and the cobra;
  you will trample the great lion and the serpent.

14 "Because he loves me," says the Lord, "I will rescue him;
  I will protect him, for he acknowledges my name.
15 He will call on me, and I will answer him;
  I will be with him in trouble,
  I will deliver him and honor him.
16 With long life I will satisfy him
  and show him my salvation."

Questions for discussion:

1) Is God's protection only needed for persecuted Christians?

2) Why do you think God allows some people to go through trials and persecution?

3) Why do some people not receive God's protection from martyrdom?

4) Do you believe you need spiritual protection? In what ways?

5) How does God use Christians in the protection of other believers or Christian workers?

6) Do you think someone can recognize divine protection or does it occur without our knowledge?

CHAPTER SEVEN:
DOES GOD COMFORT?

"...the Father of compassion and the God of all comfort, who comforts us in all our troubles,"
2 Corinthians 1:3-4

If there ever was a need for God's comfort, it was in the life of Tatyana Velkikanova. She was a 56 year old Orthodox Christian woman from Moscow who was arrested in November 1979 for what was called "anti-soviet agitation and propaganda." She was caught teaching her children the Christian faith. For this "crime" she was sentenced to four years in a labor camp followed by five years of internal exile–which is another form of imprisonment. She remained incarcerated and kept away from her family for nine years.

On December 10, 1987, one year early, she was pardoned by the Supreme Soviet. However, Mrs. Velkikanova refused to accept the pardon. By doing so she would have been admitting guilt. What she requested was a formal absolution of the so called crime for which she had been charged. The State refused, and she was returned to a labor camp to complete her sentence.

Her faith might have been simple, but it was anything but weak. She was subjected to nine years of hard labor under harsh, unsanitary conditions; enduring extremes of cold and heat, having to consume rotting food, surrounded by seriously ill people with tuberculosis and other fatal diseases. Not to waver, complain, or seek an early release, demonstrated an incredibly strong faith.

It is miraculous that believers are able to tolerate such conditions for months and years and still come out praising and thanking God. They thank God for the prison experience, because through it they obtain a greater awareness of the presence of God. These people are just normal human beings strengthened by the grace of God. They are ordinary people made extraordinary by the power of God's Holy Spirit within them. One Christian pastor threatened with prison by the authorities in Romania said, "I discovered that it was not until I was ready to die for Jesus, that I could totally live for Him. But once I was prepared to forfeit life and liberty, then I found I was ready to live, work, and serve."

Christians in prison for their faith report that they experience the miraculous comfort of God in their lives. They survive extremely long periods of incarceration under merciless conditions and suffer both physically and mentally. Many have permanent ill-health imposed upon them because of their experiences.

Without divine intervention, many more would die in prison. As bad as it is to be falsely accused and imprisoned, can you imagine the suffering of parents as they see their own children manhandled, mistreated, and even tortured in front of them? This type of thing is carried out in an attempt to force the parents to recant their Christian faith. God alone could comfort these parents, and bring any easing of their despair, as they watch their children suffer.

This scenario is not dissimilar to the inability for humans to bring comfort to others in the midst of tragedy. Many years ago, I read a book by Edward England entitled *The Mountain That Moved.* Mr. England writes about "perhaps the greatest tragedy Wales has ever known." He is referring to the Aberfan disaster.

On October 21, 1966 the village of Aberfan, a small Welsh mining village, was devastated by the landslide of a giant "slag heap," which is waste from a coal mine. The landslide covered cottages, houses, and, tragically, Pantglas Junior School. A million tons of waste crashed down on the village. The children in the school had just concluded morning prayers. One hundred and forty people died; one hundred and sixteen of them were children. Hardly a family in the village was left untouched or unscarred. Beyond the collective grief were individuals, each suffering untold personal pain. One man lost his wife and two children; children lost brothers and sisters; one man lost seven members of his family.

Bereaved parents could only think, "We did not bring our children into the world for this!" Ministers found that words were inadequate to bring comfort. One said: "There was nothing, absolutely nothing one could say, even as a minister of Jesus Christ, to these bereaved people. For the first time, some of us realized the complete inadequacy of words when we come face to face with the tragedy of life. The only meaningful language in Aberfan was the language of love... it was difficult to express the tremendous sense of privilege we had as we moved among these broken but courageous people."[1]

As Edward England so aptly points out: "What does one say to a father who has barely recognized the remains of his son?"

This kind of tragedy is repeated many times around the world. We are all too familiar with the tragedy of tsunamis, earthquakes, and hurricanes which bring flooding, mudslides, and the collapse of buildings. We are amazed by stories of incredible rescue efforts. We are saddened by hearing of people being trapped without the possibility of rescue. Hope and comfort go hand in hand. Where there is no hope, comfort is difficult to find.

Tragedies born of circumstances beyond our control are sad and heartbreaking, but tragedies intentionally caused by man are horrific. Premeditated mass murder, of whatever kind, has been a regular occurrence throughout history. One such incident took place in Beslan in September 2004.

Beslan is the small town in southern Russia where terrorists massacred 335 people, mostly children. It happened on the first day of school. There were hundreds of children and parents who were at the school to celebrate the first day of the new term. Without warning, about 40 terrorists overran the school.

The mothers and children were herded into the gymnasium. The fathers were taken outside and killed, a fact not mentioned by the media, but was borne out by the video seen on television, where only mothers and children could be seen. Consequently, some women lost their husbands *and* their children that day! All of those fathers would have been the breadwinners in the family.

The Baptist Church in the town is about 500 metres from the school. The two pastors of the church are brothers. Between their two families, they had eight children, all of whom were at the school that morning. They were each left with one child! One of them, a little girl, escaped uninjured, while the other, a boy, lost the sight in one eye and had to go to Moscow for medical treatment to save the other eye.

The two families had buried two children and then discovered another child in the morgue. The others were among the 200 children who remained unidentified until DNA samples were available from their parents. The children were burned beyond recognition. Even many of the children who escaped were so traumatized, they could not speak.

These same two pastors were called upon to minister comfort to hundreds of people in the town, while grieving so badly over the loss of their own children. How do you bring comfort into such a devastating and tragic situation? There were more than 700 families directly or indirectly affected by this mindless act. Through Eurovangelism's partners in Moscow, every family was visited and was offered assistance, love, and care, but only God could provide the real comfort needed in that horrendous circumstance.

Angels of Mercy

On one occasion, I visited Kashenko Hospital, a geriatric and psychiatric hospital in Moscow which has approximately 3,000 patients. This large and stately hospital, standing in its own grounds, was the dreaded hospital used by the KGB, Russia's Secret Police, in the harsh communist days. It was there that they performed inhumane interrogation and the torture of political and religious prisoners. Today, the place is completely different. The patients are now recipients of a ministry of comfort rarely seen elsewhere.

It all began with a few women from the Moscow Baptist Church, mostly pensioners, who went to the hospital and requested permission from the Director to allow them to visit the patients or to help out around the wards. They did not hide the fact that they were Christians. The communist Director agreed, but his motives were far from honorable. He gave them the worst possible jobs that one could find in the hospital. The place left much to be desired with regard to its cleanliness and upkeep. They were given the unenviable tasks of cleaning up the patients, cleaning the floors, and menial humiliating and objectionable jobs. They were not allowed to even speak to the patients.

The Director's idea was to teach these Christians a lesson. He intended to make their offer to help a non-event. He thought they would be gone in a few days, tired of the awfulness of the situation in which they had to work. After all, this was volunteer work! He was totally wrong in his assumption.

Not only did they continue, but their numbers increased. It grew from a few women going a couple of days a week, to over 120 women who have been carrying out their tasks at the hospital for more than ten years now. They continue to this day–but now things are very different.

Today, the Director of the hospital openly admits that

life at the hospital would be very difficult, if not impossible, if the volunteers withdrew their help and assistance. It has become a powerful and effective witness to Christian love in action. They are known as the Angels of Mercy. This ministry of comfort grew as they exercised patience over the difficult years.

Gradually, they began making contact with the patients, eventually reading to them and then praying with them. The patients began to eagerly look forward to their presence. The only help the ladies receive for this act of kindness is payment for their tram fare. These pensioners have given themselves freely to this task, and have created a ministry offering the comfort of God unsurpassed by any social service.

There are few crises in life where we do not need the comfort of God. There are times when God alone can comfort. Such was the case in Serbia. When that country was bombed by NATO forces, we received a communication from some Christian worker friends inside Serbia.

The letter said, "Things have definitely changed a lot. Hardly any cars on the road, people are in their homes or shelters. Sad, worried faces, so many questions but no answers... Why? How long? What will happen tomorrow? This morning we were awakened at 4:00 a.m. with very strong explosions right in our area. Half an hour later, another two, even closer. From the balcony of our house, we could see it all, since our home is on a hill. Heavy smoke went up to the sky. After a wake up call like that, it was not hard to stay awake. Our comfort is that nothing happens that God is not aware of, and our safest shelter is His presence... We live moment by moment in His grace."

While the bombs were falling around them, they found comfort in the sovereignty of God, knowing that nothing in life is a surprise to Him. Few of us here in North America have to live under those frightening circumstances, but whatever we face, our comfort is assured. We too can be comforted as we rest in the safety of His presence. In all circumstances, God is the God of hope. A genuine relationship with Him brings comfort, hope, and healing.

Although not all situations are outwardly critical or devastating, the desire for comfort and assurance is just as real in each one of us. I remember traveling with a colleague through four countries in Eastern Europe on one trip. In one place we stayed with a Christian family in their small home. It consisted of two rooms, a small kitchen, and a very small bathroom. One room was their everyday room in which they ate and lived, and which the parents used as a bedroom. The other room was the bedroom for the teenage son and daughter. We were given their room while the whole family slept in the day room.

In the morning, the breakfast table was laid for two people–the guests! When I enquired of my colleague as to why the family was not eating with us, he avoided giving me an answer but suggested we get on and eat the food. Later, he told me that we were actually eating their breakfast–that was all they had! Naturally, before we left, he ensured they had funds with which to purchase more food; but this highlighted for me their kindness and generosity in sharing what they had.

This family suffered at the hands of the authorities, but they spoke nothing about it. The father had been fired from his position as a mathematics teacher at the local high school because he would not renounce his faith and give up his association with the local church. Their son wanted to go to university and the daughter to college. Both had been refused the opportunity for further education because of the Christian stand taken by the family. The father attempted to feed his family by making window frames in a small shed he had erected in the garden. Such were the restrictions upon them for living out their Christian faith.

They were a happy family, not complaining about their hardship and the difficulties they encountered. Their devotion to the Lord left an indelible impression on me that their faith was strong. They lived in the comfort and assurance which only God could provide. They literally rested on the promises of God, which had proven true over and over again. Over the years of persecution, they had come to appreciate and understand the true values of life; and they were not the values found in the West.

The God of all Comfort

It is not until we are pressed to the wall through crises that we discover what is important in life. What really matters rises to the surface. We quickly learn that our family and our relationships are of extreme importance. When we face serious illness or the death of a loved one, peripheral matters of work, money and possessions, become just that-peripheral. Relationships become important, and no more so than a relationship with God our Father. At that time, we need strength and comfort. Under those circumstances He alone can bring that real deep comfort and consolation we need. I heard it once said that a crisis in life can be the anvil upon which the human spirit is shaped, or it can be the hammer which crushes the spirit. It depends upon how we respond. How we respond is determined by the confidence and assurance which comes from our relationship with God, our heavenly Father.

Many years ago, I read an article by Helen Crawford entitled "The God of All Comfort." In it she described her battle with illness and a broken relationship with one of her children. At one point, she was in hospital about to have an operation. During the night prior to the medical procedure, she remembers waking up in a cold sweat with the terrible repetitious thought going through her mind, "I have cancer! I have cancer!" She went on to say that it was followed by the ministry of God's Spirit as He brought to mind a modern version of Proverbs 31:18 which states, "My lamp of faith and dependence upon God need not go out, but full of the oil of His Spirit it can burn on through the night of trouble, privation, and sorrow, warning away such robbers as fear, doubt, and distrust." She immediately was left with a sense of warmth, peace, and a calmness which had replaced the prior fear and cold. She said, "This was 'my night' but God was removing 'the robbers.'"[2]

The psalmist expressed a similar sentiment when he reiterated that, "in God I trust; I will not be afraid" (Psalm 56:11). Resting in the promises of God and trusting in His faithfulness to His Word brings comfort to us in our distress. Just as it was for Helen Crawford, so it is for every believer; the Word of God is first in providing comfort. In fact, the book of Psalms is usually the first place we turn in Scripture for words of comfort and consolation. The Holy Spirit will also bring to mind an appropriate Scriptural passage or verse. Hence the necessity of reading, learning, and studying the Scriptures so they may be recalled when needed.

Fear instigates the need for comfort. Some fears are rational, others irrational, but all fear, nonetheless, can be eradicated by the comfort of God. You may remember that it was John who wrote, "There is no fear in love. But perfect love drives out fear" (John 4:18). God's love is perfect. Therefore, it is His love alone which is the antidote to fear. Out of God's love comes His comfort.

How is it that we can be comforted through those dreaded medical procedures and operations? How is it that we can be comforted at the loss of a spouse or close friend? What about when we lose our job or the world crashes in upon us financially–how do we receive comfort and strength then? We feel devastated, and we are!

Yet God has His own way of bringing us the comfort we need. Sometimes it is subtle, other times it is open and obvious. Using His Word and using His people, God provides the right message at the right time. As believers, we are encouraged in the Scripture to "Rejoice with those who rejoice; mourn with those who mourn" (Romans 12:15). This is the way that the Holy Spirit works through other people.

Romans 8:28 is probably one of the most quoted verses from Scripture–and not always at the most appropriate of times. I know well-meaning Christians who have quoted this verse to people believing that they are ministering comfort, but it fact, it proved to be most unhelpful. It can be the right text, but given at the wrong moment.

I know a pastor who, having just lost his wife, stated

that, "If anyone else quotes Romans 8:28 to me, I shall scream at them!" The sense of the text is essentially saying that what has occurred has happened for our good, and that in the end, all will be well. However, there are times when we find it hard to readily agree with that sentiment. Yet we must never lose confidence in the sovereignty of God. Looking at most events in our lives retrospectively, we see that the outcome is often far different from what we might have expected, and then we can admit that the verse from Romans certainly had its application.

When Jesus was about to end His ministry here on earth, He told the disciples that although He would be gone, they would not be alone. He said that He would send the Counsellor or Comforter to them. He was, of course, referring to the coming of the Holy Spirit. The meaning of Comforter in this setting was "one who comes alongside," and this is exactly what the Holy Spirit does. He comes alongside us in our times of crisis to bring us comfort and strength. In fact, when looking back on an event, it is not uncommon for people to be amazed at the strength and grace they received, just at the time it was needed. I distinctly remember that this was my experience as I went for the removal of a tumor. There was no way, humanly speaking, that I could have had the calmness and confidence I had, unless given the comfort and strength by the Spirit of God. This, of course, was the result of other believers praying for just such comfort. This is the same for all those believers who suffered horrendously at the hands of persecutors. We cannot understand how they lived through their interrogation, torture, and long imprisonment. It was only by the strength and comfort given through the ministry of God's Spirit.

Yet as God provides us comfort, it brings with it a certain responsibility. Paul explains what this responsibility is in his letter to the Corinthians. He says that we are comforted so that we might comfort. He says, "Praise be to the God and Father of our Lord Jesus Christ, the Father of compassion and the God of all comfort, who comforts us in all our troubles, so that we can comfort those in any trouble with the comfort we ourselves have received from God. For just as the sufferings of Christ flow over into our lives, so also through Christ our comfort overflows" (2 Corinthians 1:3-5). I am reminded of the many people who have suffered horrendously in life but have been used incredibly by God to minister comfort to thousands of other sufferers. How privileged we are to serve a God of all comfort. As His children, we can be assured of that comfort; and we can live in the truth that "weeping may remain for a night but rejoicing comes in the morning" (Psalm 30:5).

GUIDE FOR GROUP STUDY

Chapter 7: Does God Comfort?

Bible reading: 2 Corinthians 1:3-7

3 Praise be to the God and Father of our Lord Jesus Christ, the Father of compassion and the God of all comfort, 4 who comforts us in all our troubles, so that we can comfort those in any trouble with the comfort we ourselves receive from God. 5 For just as we share abundantly in the sufferings of Christ, so also our comfort abounds through Christ. 6 If we are distressed, it is for your comfort and salvation; if we are comforted, it is for your comfort, which produces in you patient endurance of the same sufferings we suffer. 7 And our hope for you is firm, because we know that just as you share in our sufferings, so also you share in our comfort.

Questions for discussion:

1) What situations call for God's comfort?

2) Share an experience of God's comfort in your life or in the life of a loved one.

3) What else does God bring into our lives along with His comfort?

4) According to Scripture, how are we benefitted when we receive God's comfort?

5) How do we share God's comfort with others?

6) What skills do you believe are necessary in order for someone to minister well in the area of comforting others?

CHAPTER EIGHT:
DOES GOD INTERVENE?

"And we know that in all things God works for the good of those who love him."
Romans 8:28

A number of years ago I was in Vancouver, Canada for a missions conference. While there, I was scheduled to speak at a church in Maple Ridge, about one hour's drive east of Vancouver. The arrangement was that I would take the train to a certain station and then would be picked up by car. I left the hotel at 7:30 a.m. on the Sunday morning and walked across the road to take the train. The station was locked. The sign on the gates indicated that the first train would leave just before 9:00 a.m. The first church service started at 9:00 a.m. I returned to the hotel and called the pastor to inform him of the situation. He was somewhat at a loss as to the answer. He decided that there was no alternative but to make the one hour drive into Vancouver to pick me up. He left home immediately and arrived at the hotel one hour later, soon after 8:30 a.m. He had informed the associate pastor that we would be late, and that they should proceed without us. At least we would be well in time for the second service and maybe in time to speak at the first.

As we left the hotel, the pastor committed the journey to the Lord in prayer. The weather was damp with mist and early morning fog. Together we commiserated about the situation while the pastor drove steadily and diligently through the fog. We ignored the time as we chatted together. As we pulled into the church parking lot, we looked at our watches. We were absolutely amazed. The time was 8:55 a.m.; well in time for the first service. I was totally bemused knowing how long it had taken the pastor to drive into Vancouver. We had returned in less than half the time. The pastor continuously repeated, "I can't understand it! I can't understand it!" Did God intervene to move us along supernaturally? Was what I had to say to that congregation *that* important? We shall never know.

As we have already seen from the many stories in the lives of different people, many events are so extraordinary that there can be no other explanation except for divine intervention.

In the book *The God who Changes Lives*, edited by Mark Elsdon-Dew, there is a story about a girl named Philippa Dudgeon who worked with the Eastern European Bible Mission in Holland. She wanted to attend her cousin's twenty-first birthday celebration in England, especially knowing how much her family wanted her there. The nearest airport to where she was working was Antwerp, Belgium. It had been hard for her to find enough money for the air ticket back to England, but she had achieved it, and looked forward to being with her family. She boarded the bus for the airport, sat down and immediately fell asleep.

At the airport, she left the bus and made her way to the check-in counter. Looking at her ticket, the attendant pointed out that her ticket was from Antwerp, and that she was in the Brussels Airport. Antwerp was 25 miles north. She had taken the wrong bus. Her ticket was a "special" ticket which could not be changed and it was too late to travel to the next airport. All she could do was call out to God for help. It was simply, "Lord, help! What do I do?" Into her mind came the words, "My grace is sufficient for you, and my power is made perfect in your weakness!" She knew God would intervene.

As she stood in the middle of the concourse with her luggage, she began praising God with her favourite song, "You are My Hiding Place," realizing she needed to know the reality of that song at that moment. After twenty minutes, a man approached her and asked for her ticket. He left with her ticket and returned a few minutes later with her ticket stamped with red mark. On enquiring what this meant, he said that they were going to fly her to Antwerp. As the man rushed her through passport control, a voice over the public address system called, "Would Miss Dudgeon please go to Gate 52 where there is a plane waiting."

Arriving at the gate, she was met by the pilot who helped with the luggage and ushered her onto the plane. Five flight attendants were the only occupants of the plane. She was the only passenger on this Boeing 737!

As they prepared for take-off the pilot announced, "Good afternoon lady passenger. This is your captain speaking! We will be in the air for seven minutes before landing at Antwerp Airport. Enjoy the flight."[1] As Philippa sat back in her seat she simply praised God for His intervention. She said that it confirmed to her that God is alive! However, she felt the main reason He provided the way out for her was because He loved her. She knew Him to be a God who answers prayer.

Does God really do these things? Or are we just the recipients of constant coincidences? We cannot always answer precisely the difficult questions regarding God's actions, but we can rest in the knowledge that He is there, He does act, He does care, and He certainly intervenes when the time is right for Him.

We cannot understand the timetable of God, but we trust that His timing is always perfect. When we see how He has provided, in what we might call "the nick of time," we come to realize that usually, that is God's time–never too early and never too late. The help comes at the moment we need it. The answer comes at the moment we need it. God promises His presence will always be with us. He provides strength for the here and now. His grace is sufficient for today, as it will be also for tomorrow.

It used to be said that you could not be a Christian in Eastern Europe and not believe in miracles. Out of necessity, the church, under pressure from any government, finds itself relying heavily upon divine intervention and guidance. Unfortunately, in the West we have a tendency to rely upon our human ingenuity and resources first. Then, if that doesn't work, we decide perhaps God should be let in on the project to see if He has any ideas or can make some contribution. It's a tragedy that we wait until we reach that stage before we think seriously about going to God and allowing Him to act.

Through its seventy years of persecution, the Church in Eastern Europe learned such dependence on God. As we have seen in this book, their expectancy of His intervention caused miracles to become part of their everyday life. Events happened which could not be explained away. Sadly, there are people who do not wish to acknowledge the hand of God touching lives, and will consider these unusual occurrences as pure coincidence. Most Christians would classify them as God-incidences, rather than coincidences. The mathematical probability of chance in all of these stories would be of astronomical proportions.

So we ask the question, "Does God really intervene in our affairs?" I believe He does if we let Him. This quiet assurance comes from knowing Who is in control and from understanding the sovereignty of God. Proverbs tells us, "The fear of the Lord is the beginning of wisdom, and the knowledge of the Holy One is understanding" (Proverbs 9:10). Having spiritual wisdom and understanding is required of us, if we are to make sense of the many "coincidences" in the Christian life.

Does God Always Intervene?

It seems not. I think the most moving experience of my life was a visit I made to Auschwitz Concentration Camp in Poland. The two hour tour of the camp was a very sobering time. The tons of human hair, personal belongings, suitcases and shoes, brought me face to face with the stark reality of what this concentration camp had meant to the thousands upon thousands of men, women, and children who found themselves on the one-way road to a barbarous death. I, along with three friends, stood in the gas chambers where thousands of people died. We saw the ovens where their bodies were cremated. The experience left us virtually speechless. Few words can express the emotional response to such an evil and meaningless deed.

One of the most evil dictators in recent living memory was Nicolae Ceauşescu of Romania. After he and his wife were executed by their own soldiers on Christmas Day 1989, the world was given the opportunity to see some of his legacy. The Romanian orphans became an international news item. The children had been placed in mansion-like decrepit buildings, with few facilities and little attention. The extreme cold conditions in the winter gave way to sweltering heat in the summer.

We might question why there were more than 150,000 children in these homes. It was because Ceauşescu wanted to increase the Romanian population to 30 million from 23 million. In his attempt to do so, he issued an edict which stated that all women of child-bearing age would have, at least, four children. He even had officials monitoring pregnancies to ensure they were brought to full term. The outcome was that many women had children they could not afford to keep or care for, and simply had to abandon them to these homes.

The children were segregated into homes by age; babies up to three years old, children three to six years of age, and then six years to teenagers. Workers were so few that one took care of 25 to 30 children. As a consequence, the children just laid in their cribs staring at the ceiling; unattended, unloved, unheld, soaked by their own urine, changed once a day, and fed strictly by the clock. They were treated no better, if not worse, than animals in a zoo. Many of the children were emotionally disturbed, psychologically damaged, and mentally underdeveloped because of the lack of stimulation from not being handled, loved, or cared for.

There were two year olds unable to sit up and three year olds unable to walk or talk. When Westerners were allowed into the rooms, little arms reached out to be held, to be touched, to be loved. In some centers there was no running water for more than a week at a time, and no wood for the stoves, used for heat and cooking. In the homes for the handicapped, there were rooms for the "irrecoverable children" and other rooms for the "hyperactive," where the children were tied to the metal-framed beds. Such was the inhumane treatment of little children who did not ask to be born, but were abandoned once they arrived into this world.

Dare we join our voices with many others who said, "Where was God when all this happened?" Sometimes we can come to terms with natural disasters more easily than we can with evil dictators subjecting fellow human beings to torture or to an inhumane existence. How is it that the dictators live in luxurious mansions, while their subjugated population simply subsists, or lives in abject poverty? These are actions of injustice which we all abhor.

Man's heart is evil and he will make decisions and take action motivated by his inner being. "Power corrupts," Lord Acton once said, "and absolute power corrupts absolutely!" Most dictators fall under the spell of power and position; their actions displaying the evil within their hearts.

When men reject, ignore, and refuse to obey God, the result will always be self-adulation and atrocious inhumanity. As man refuses to acknowledge that God is alive, then God is not called upon to intervene. It is a small wonder that man's corruption and greed reap such havoc in our society. Havoc comes when man considers violence to be the means to an end.

A radio interviewer asked the question, "Where was God on September 11, 2001?" (The date of the terrorist attack on the twin towers in New York)

The guest replied, "Why should we expect God to have been there when we have asked Him to leave our schools, our places of government and business, and our society in general?"

For Christians, life is different. We have already experienced the intervening work of God's Spirit as He orchestrated events and situations to bring us face to face with the reality of His existence. It may have been the sudden loss of a friend or relative through an accident, or at the funeral which followed. It may have been a serious illness within the family, or perhaps relationship problems which caused some introspection, and the questioning of life and the reality of God. It's during those times that God's Spirit begins to create a spiritual awareness. The fact that God is alive becomes very real when we see Him changing lives. God takes the ordinary and makes it extraordinary.

Look at the lives God changes. Humanly speaking, we would think it impossible for some folks who are so strung out on drugs and addicted to alcohol to ever be changed and renewed. Yet God is the God of the impossible. God intervenes as only God can. He causes miraculous recoveries. When we fully understand the redemption bought by Christ's death on the cross, which satisfied the justice and wrath of God, then we begin to comprehend the unlimited depths to which God's grace, love, and redemption can reach.

God is at work in the lives of people, bringing salvation and extraordinary changes along with it. The story of Svetlana from Serbia illustrates this very point. She says, "Since my earliest days I have always felt worthless. My mother abandoned me the moment I was born. Other people took care of me, but didn't really want me. As a baby I was often left in a cold room by myself. Eventually my aunt felt sorry for me and took me in. I was raised by her just a few houses away from my mother, but she never wanted to have contact with me. Because of this, I considered my mother an enemy and became embittered against her. All this made me very discontented with my life and angry with the whole world, creating a huge gap between me and other people.

"I sought help from the Novi Sad Christian Fellowship (Novi Sad, Serbia). There they showed me that my Heavenly Father loves me unconditionally, and accepts me just as I am. My heart found peace in Him. Now I love people and I have a desire to help everyone. My friends, family and acquaintances have seen a change in me and dozens of them have also come to know Christ as their Savior. Among these is my own mother to whom I was finally able to say, 'I love you.' Christ has healed my heart and has bridged the gap that existed between me and others."

Whether it is to bring us salvation, to change our lives, or just to confirm His love for us, God intervenes in all manners of ways. Consider the following simple story.

In one of the Alpha program videos, there is a story about an American pastor named Carl Tuttle who came from a broken home. Abuse from his father caused him to have a very unhappy childhood. One day, after becoming a Christian, he decided he wanted to hear God speak and find out what God was saying to him. He felt he really needed to hear from God personally. He left his house and drove into the country where he could spend some quiet, uninterrupted time alone with God. He found a convenient location and began to pray. He did not pray for too long before he became discouraged. He felt he was making no progress in his exercise to hear God. So he returned home feeling somewhat down and disappointed.

Arriving home, he told his wife that he would go in to see their two month old baby, Zachary. He picked up the baby and at the same time felt an overwhelming sense of love for his child. In fact, he began to weep. As he did so, he started talking to his son. He found himself saying, "Zachary, I love you. I love you with all my heart. No matter what happens in this life, I will never harm you, I'll always protect you. I'll always be your father, I'll always be your friend, I'll always care for you, I'll always nurture you and I'll do this, no matter what sins you commit, no matter what you do, no matter whether you turn from me or from God."

Suddenly things changed. Carl felt that he personally was in God's arms and that God was speaking to him and saying, "Carl, you are my son and I love you. No matter what you do, no matter where you go, I'll always care for you. I'll always provide for you, I'll always guide you."[2]

He didn't hear God speak audibly, but he certainly sensed God speaking to him. In that moment, God confirmed to him that he was His child, that He cared for him, and that He would take care of him. He felt loved. He felt special. God communicates His love and care in various ways. God certainly intervened in the life of Carl Tuttle that day.

Our individual situations are unique. We might think that there is no answer to our particular crisis but, as we have already indicated, God is the God of the impossible. With God, there is no such thing as a hopeless case. The word hopeless does not exist in the Divine vocabulary. Our situations might appear hopeless, but with God, nothing is impossible. We have real hope in Him, which brings purpose, motivation, and enthusiasm. God made you, therefore God cares for you.

However imperfect we think we are has no bearing on how God looks at us or on His care for us. We have nothing to offer Him, but He loves us just the same. We don't have to impress God. God accepts us just we are. We have no capacity to improve ourselves for presentation to God. He knows us through and through, so all our efforts to impress Him are futile. Remember that you are important; to yourself, to others, and especially to God. If you are a child of God then He has chosen you, adopted you, and accepted you. Does that not make you special in His eyes?

God's most important intervention came when He broke into history, bringing us the incarnation. If God had not intervened in our diabolical situation, then mankind would have remained in a state of eternal condemnation. But God provided the solution to sin and rebellion by sending Jesus as a baby in Bethlehem. Incredibly, God placed that condemnation on His Son, Jesus Christ, who totally bore the wrath of God and the justice of God against sin in His death on the cross. If God exercised such unconditional love to us then, why would we ever question His intervention in our lives now?

Do We Limit God's Intervention?

The thought is not new, but do we experience only what we expect of God? If we don't see miracles, is it because we don't *expect* to see miracles? If we don't see God's intervention in our lives is it because we don't anticipate it? If this is the case, then it is a sad reflection on our understanding of the sovereignty of God. Either God is sovereign or He is not. He cannot be half-sovereign. He cannot be sovereign in one aspect of life and not another. He cannot be sovereign in creation and not sovereign in the lives of His children. Surely God, as the almighty God, can intervene in our lives as He chooses. His ability to do so should never be in question. It would be tragic to discover that the intervention of God in our lives is restricted by our own thinking, our understanding, or even our lack of faith.

Whether we are looking for healing, for guidance, for comfort, or any other aspect of God's intervention in our lives, we are encouraged to look in the right place. We have been given the Word of God so that God can speak through it. We have been given the privileged channel of prayer by which we can share with Him our devotion, our worship, our thanksgiving, and our supplications. We have been given the ministry of God's Spirit within our lives to guide us in all areas. The Spirit of God is also the one who plants the gift of faith within us, so that we might look expectantly for God to work. We ask, and then we wait. The waiting is the most difficult part.

What do we know about "waiting on God?" Whatever blessing or divine intervention we are seeking from God, it requires some element of waiting upon Him. We are often so busy doing the legitimate things of life, even Christian service, that we leave this kind of spiritual exercise until times of extreme need or crisis. We are recipients of the benefits of God's grace on a daily basis. As John says, "From the fullness of his grace we have all received one blessing after another" (John 1:16); but I am referring to more than our daily blessings. I am referring to God's divine intervention into specific situations–situations where we desperately need to see and experience His intervention. In these weighty circumstances, we are called to a concerted exercise of waiting upon God.

How is this accomplished? We must set aside deliberate time to speak with God and allow Him to speak with us. The attitude of our hearts and our spiritual disposition must be right. We approach God in humility, realizing who He is, and who we are. It is right that we come to God as His children, but we also come with a servant heart. We do not demand from God. We cannot dictate to God; that is not our right. We do not negotiate with God. We lay out before Him our hopes and desires and, like Jesus in the garden of Gethsemane, we also submit to the Father's will. If we offer a servant heart, then we offer our obedience. Into such a setting God can speak and act.

Commit your life and situation to God, and then watch Him intervene. Look for Him to right the wrongs, to heal the relationships, to remove the frustrations, and ease the pain. God does not force Himself upon us, but as we go to Him and express our need in a child-like simple faith, He will respond; and often in ways we could not even imagine.

Our situations are no surprise to Him. He has not abandoned us. He loves us unconditionally. We need to pray that He will work out the situation for the blessing of ourselves and others, and that ultimately it will bring Him glory. During Jesus' ministry, He touched the eyes of two blind men and said, "According to your faith will it be done to you" (Matthew 9:29). How we wish we were always like those men. Their request for healing was granted because of their evident faith.

As you wait patiently for God's intervention into your life, you may find times where your faith needs help. In those moments, recall the lesson learned in Mark chapter 9. In this passage, there is a man whose child needs healing. The disciples tried to heal the boy, and failed. Jesus steps into the picture. He tells those who are there that they are an "unbelieving generation."

The man says to Jesus, "If you can do anything, take pity on us and help us."

Jesus couldn't believe the man gave him an "if"! "IF you can?" Jesus exclaims. (emphasis mine)

Don't approach God with an "if" in your heart. Approach boldly and learn the lesson Jesus then taught: "Everything is possible for him who believes."

The man knew he needed help with his "if." He asked Jesus, "I do believe; help me overcome my unbelief!"

I pray this book has encouraged you that what man has termed "coincidence" is nothing short of God's perfect timing. I pray you will have open eyes and an open heart to see God at work around you, every day. And if your unbelief needs help, I pray you will pray the prayer of the man in Mark 9. When you rid your belief of the word "if," you will be positioned to experience God like never before.

GUIDE FOR GROUP STUDY

Chapter 8: Does God Intervene?

Bible reading: Romans 8:16-27

16 The Spirit himself testifies with our spirit that we are God's children. 17 Now if we are children, then we are heirs—heirs of God and co-heirs with Christ, if indeed we share in his sufferings in order that we may also share in his glory.

18 I consider that our present sufferings are not worth comparing with the glory that will be revealed in us. 19 For the creation waits in eager expectation for the children of God to be revealed. 20 For the creation was subjected to frustration, not by its own choice, but by the will of the one who subjected it, in hope 21 that the creation itself will be liberated from its bondage to decay and brought into the freedom and glory of the children of God.

22 We know that the whole creation has been groaning as in the pains of childbirth right up to the present time. 23 Not only so, but we ourselves, who have the firstfruits of the Spirit, groan inwardly as we wait eagerly for our adoption to sonship, the redemption of our bodies. 24 For in this hope we were saved. But hope that is seen is no hope at all. Who hopes for what they already have? 25 But if we hope for what we do not yet have, we wait for it patiently.

26 In the same way, the Spirit helps us in our weakness. We do not know what we ought to pray for, but the Spirit himself intercedes for us through wordless groans. 27 And he who searches our hearts knows the mind of the Spirit, because the Spirit intercedes for God's people in accordance with the will of God.

Questions for discussion:

1) If you have accepted Jesus Christ as your Savior, share your experience of God's intervention at the moment of your conversion.

2) What areas of your life have been directly impacted by God's intervention?

3) In what ways does God intervene on behalf of His children?

4) Can we, or should we, always expect God to intervene in our situations? How?

5) Why do you think God might not intervene if you ask Him to?

6) What should we learn from God's intervention in our lives?

REFERENCES

Chapter Two
[1] C.S. Lewis in *Letters to an American Lady*, copyright 1967 by Wm. B. Eerdmans Publishing Co.
[2] "How Prayer Made Me a Father Again" by Richard Whetstone in *Chicken Soup for the Soul*, copyright 2003 by Health Communications Inc.
[3] "Footprints in the Sand" by Margaret Fishback Powers, written in 1964.

Chapter Three
[1] Carmen Benson in *What About Those of Us Who Are Not Healed?* Copyright 1975 by Logos International.
[2] Ibid.
[3] Ibid.
[4] *New Life in Serbia* by Vera and Danny Kuranji, used by permission.

Chapter Four
[1] *Questions of Life* by Nicky Gumbel, copyright by Nicky Gumbel 1993. Published by Kingsway Publications Ltd., U.K. Used by permission. Nicky Gumbel is relating Michael Bordeaux's story from *Risen Indeed*, published in 1983 by Darton, Longman Todd.

Chapter Five
[1] "Seeking First the Kingdom," article by Roger Steer which appeared in *Discipleship Journal*, Issue Thirty-one, 1985.
[2] Ibid.

Chapter Seven

[1] Edward England in *The Mountain That Moved*, copyright 1967 by Save the Children Fund. Published by Wm. B. Eerdmans Publishing Co.

[2] "The God of All Comfort" article by Helen Crawford which appeared in *Discipleship Journal*, Issue Thirty-one, in 1985.

Chapter Eight

[1] *The God Who Changes Lives* (Volume One); edited by Mark Elsdon-Dew, copyright 1995 by HTB Publications.

[2] *How Can I Be Sure of My Faith?* Alpha Video Series issued by HTB, London, U.K. Used by permission.

ALSO BY JOHN MURRAY

Real Faith
What's at the heart of the Gospel?

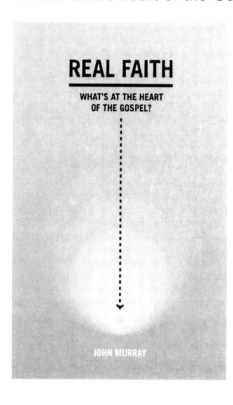

Real Faith is an asset to the library of anyone who is serious about understanding the foundations of the Christian faith.

Written in a style that is easily understandable, inviting, and genuine, the reader will come away with a deeper knowledge about what it means to be a Christian.

ISBN: 978-1-6202004-2-1
Order through the author's website or your local Christian bookstore.

Connect with John Murray:
http://jmurray.ca
http://www.facebook.com/AuthorJohnMurray
Twitter: @AuthorJMurray

CPSIA information can be obtained at www.ICGtesting.com
Printed in the USA
LVOW10s2258031014

407192LV00001B/1/P